Opening the Town Hall Door

An Introduction to Local Government

Jane Hutt

BSP

Bedford Square Press

Published by
BEDFORD SQUARE PRESS of the
National Council for Voluntary Organisations
26 Bedford Square, London WC1B 3HU

First published 1988
Second edition 1990

Typeset by BookEns, Saffron Walden, Essex

Printed and bound in Great Britain by
J. W. Arrowsmith Ltd., Bristol

British Library Cataloguing in Publication Data
Hutt, Jane
    Opening the town hall door: an introduction to local
    government. – 2nd. ed. – Practical guides. National
    Council for Voluntary Organisations.
    1. Great Britain. Local government
    I. Title
    352.041

ISBN 0-7199-1278-4

OPEN DOOR

An Introduction to Local Government

Jane Hutt has lived and worked in Wales for 18 years. In the early 1970s she was a community worker in the south Wales valleys and towns. She then worked for 11 years as co-ordinator of Welsh Women's Aid, setting up a network of refuges throughout Wales. She became a county councillor in 1981, serving an inner city area of Cardiff, and has chaired the council's Women's Committee. As a councillor she helped to set up a training workshop for women providing free courses in microelectronics and computing. She has taught social administration and community work in local universities and colleges, and is the first director of the Tenant Participation Advisory Service in Wales.

Contents

CONTENTS

Acknowledgements

I should like to thank Welsh Women's Aid for publishing an earlier version of *Opening the Town Hall Door*, on which this revised, updated and extended version is based.

I should also like to thank the many people from both inside and outside local government who gave freely of their knowledge and experience, in particular Michael Trickey, for his contribution to the section on local government finance.

Finally, I should like to thank Richard Gutch, Assistant Director (Local Voluntary Action Department), NCVO, for acting as consultant to this project and for his comments, amendments and valuable contribution to this guide.

1
Introduction

Everyone comes into contact with local councils, since they provide the majority of public services we use in our everyday lives. In addition, many people have dealings with local councils when they get involved in voluntary organisations and community groups and campaign about an issue which affects a group of people or a neighbourhood where the local authority is responsible for providing a service or amenity. Some people may also wish to apply for a grant from their local councils to enable them to run a service or organise an event. For all these reasons, it is important to understand how local government is organised, and how it works.

The organisation of local government is complicated and often mystifying to people who are trying find out who their local councillors are, or who they should contact to find about sources of funding, or how they can make a complaint or lobby for a change in the policy of their local authority. Voluntary organisations and action groups can spend many months trying to disentangle the maze of bureaucracy that seems to exist in making applications for funds, and individual citizens may have an even tougher time in attempting to redress a grievance or take some steps to obtain services which they need at a particular time in their lives. Others are not aware of the services they are entitled to receive from their local councils or their rights of challenge or appeal if the local authority is using laws or implementing policies which affect them.

Added to all this are the constant changes in local government which are taking place due to the introduction of new laws which affect the services, structure and responsibilities of local authorities.

In the past 10 years there have been over 50 separate pieces of legislation concerning local government, ranging from the abolition of the Greater London Council (GLC) and metropolitan county councils (MCCs) to the introduction of competitive tendering for certain council services. The financing of local government has been radically changed with the abolition of the rates and the introduction of the poll tax (community charge). Restrictions on local authority spending have been a feature of the present government's policies affecting the level and quality of services provided. These have been closely accompanied by legislative measures to remove from local government the responsibility for providing many of the local services we have taken for granted as belonging to the public sector – particularly in our education and housing services. The government has clearly sought to change the role of local government in the past 10 years as far as the provision of services is concerned – giving local authorities more of an 'enabling and monitoring' role in the provision of services rather than as the chief providers of local services. Increasing financial controls have been clearly tied into a policy of increasing the power of central government to decide what should be provided by local government and how it should be provided.

The increasing intervention of central government in local decision making has extended to areas where local authorities have traditionally been able to decide for themselves what policies and directions they would like to take, for example, in commenting on the effect of government policies and funding projects which may be directly critical of the government. The government has attempted through recent and current legislation to control and restrict local government in the exercise of its functions, in its funding of voluntary bodies and community groups, in its attempts to promote equal opportunities and in its freedom to decide locally what should be the quality and level of service provided. In an attempt to lessen the ability of local authorities to work and act 'politically' in promoting policies which may have been endorsed by the electorate through the ballot box, the government has also introduced restrictions on those who work for local authorities and stand as elected Members.

The new edition of *Opening the Town Hall Door* charts all the major changes of the past 10 years. Many of the most significant changes have been brought in or implemented in the present

Session of this government since the 1987 General Election. The implications of the 1988 Local Government Act and the 1989 Local Government and Housing Act are dealt with in detail as they affect our local services – their delivery, who controls them, who finances them and what role local government has left to play as they are implemented.

Opening the Town Hall Door has a wider role to play than was originally envisaged in the first edition published in 1987. The central purpose of the book has been to shed some light on how local government works for the benefit of individual citizens, voluntary organisations and community groups. It explains the way decisions are made by local authorities, including the influence of party political groups in local government. It suggests ways in which you can most effectively lobby your local council and councillors, as well as taking you through the steps of applying for a grant and indicating the sources of funding still available through local authorities. It deals with complaints, the role and powers of the local government ombudsman and your rights in taking action through the courts and tribunals. In the new edition it also includes a chapter on your rights to personal information held by local authorities and looks at your rights to privacy with the newly established poll tax registers. The book aims to act as a guide for those who want to try and break down the barriers which still exist between many local authorities and the people they serve and represent. It aims to provide useful reading for those who wish to contribute to the 'opening up' of local government, as well as for those in the community who want to have more of an influence on the way their local councils make decisions affecting their lives.

The book now has an important additional function in the light of recent government legislation affecting local government. As well as outlining all the major changes of the past 10 years it reveals the need for new thinking in how we can ensure that our local services are accountable and accessible. The need to develop partnerships in supporting, improving and developing our local services has never been greater with the increased centralisation of government control over local authorities. The confusion about the miriad of changes which surround local government must be unravelled in order to ensure that local people have a say in local services which they use and depend upon.

Throughout the book, references will be made to the advice

and support which is available from the National Council for Voluntary Organisations (NCVO), the Scottish Council for Voluntary Organisations (SCVO) and the Wales Council for Voluntary Action (WCVA) as well as other organisations such as the Local Government Information Unit (LGIU) which can assist voluntary organisations and community groups in understanding many of the changes we have described and can also aid and assist groups in their dealings with local authorities. (Their addresses are listed in Appendix 1.)

NOTE

Although this guide deals with the structure and responsibilities of local government in England and Wales, many of its contents will be relevant and useful to people living in Scotland and Northern Ireland in terms of the way local governemnt works and how voluntary organisations and individuals can attempt to influence it.

The terms 'local councils' and 'local authorities' will be used interchangeably throughout this guide.

2
Structure and Responsibilities of Local Government in England and Wales

Local government has gone through a major upheaval since 1986 with the abolition of the Greater London Council (GLC) and the metropolitan county councils (MCCs). This chapter will outline the structure of local government since the changes in 1986, explaining the different types of local authorities in England and Wales, how they fit in with each other and what they are responsible for.

It will also explain the functions and areas of responsibilities of the many joint boards and authorities which have been set up since the abolition of the MCCs and GLC.

2.1 Structure

Local government is divided up into levels or 'tiers' of local authorities which have responsibility for providing different types of services, covering different geographical areas. The ways in which these services are divided between the councils in an area will vary depending on what part of England or Wales you live in.

This chapter will describe who is responsible for what, so that you know, for example, that if you live in a 'shire' county area, the county council will be responsible for providing social services and education, but the district council, which covers a smaller area than the county, will be responsible for housing and environmental (public) health. However, if you live in inner London, your London borough has been responsible for social services, housing, environmental health and education since April 1990 with the abolition of the Inner London Education Authority.

The different levels and types of local authorities cover separate geographical areas. You may live in a town or village where there are two major local councils operating in your area but they are entirely separate. They are housed in different buildings, each with their own paid staff and elected councillors. They have separate powers, responsibilities, budgets and elections. In your town or city, you may have a City Hall or Civic Centre, where the borough council is based. You may also have a County Hall where your county council is based. The county council will cover a much larger geographical area than the district council and, as has been said, will exercise different responsibilities.

It can be confusing to find that your local borough councillor may also be a county councillor, or your local community councillor may also be a district or borough councillor. However, their responsibilities and powers are entirely separate in relation to the different councils they serve on.

It is important to approach your local authorities separately and not assume that if one gives you support, the other automatically will. The councils in your area may be controlled by different political parties (see section 4.1) and they have different responsibilities, policies and budgets.

As has been discussed in the introduction, new laws affecting local government services introduced since the 1987 General Election have resulted in some council services being put out to tender and others – such as housing and education – facing changes under the Education Reform Act 1988 and the Housing

Act 1988. This has meant that local authorities may not always be the bodies actually delivering the service even though they have overall responsibility for the provision of local services in the area. These changes will be dealt with fully under 2.3, Recent changes in local authority service provision.

It is helpful to divide England and Wales into five parts in explaining the structure of local government:

a) *the non-metropolitan areas* (see map)

b) *the metropolitan areas* (see map)

c) *the London boroughs* (see map)

d) *joint boards*

e) *parish, town and community councils*

A) NON-METROPOLITAN AREAS

If we look at the non-metropolitan areas first, we have two major levels of local government:

- *county councils* (known as shire counties) (39 in England and 8 in Wales)
- d*istrict councils* (also known as borough or city councils) (269 in England and 57 in Wales)

B) METROPOLITAN AREAS

If we then look at the metropolitan areas, the metropolitan districts have responsibility for most local authority functions, but they are grouped together in six metropolitan areas. These bring together the metropolitan districts in – Greater Manchester, Merseyside, South Yorkshire, Tyne and Wear, West Midlands and West Yorkshire, which used to form the MCCs.

- *Metropolitan district councils*
  These are the district councils operating within the six metropolitan areas. There are 36 in England.

C) LONDON BOROUGHS AND ILEA

As far as London is concerned, there are 32 boroughs, 12 of which are 'inner' London boroughs and 20 of which are 'outer' London boroughs. (There is also the City of London which is a corporation elected by residents and businesses in the City of London area.)

The ILEA was abolished under the Education Reform Act 1988 in April 1990. The functions of the ILEA have been taken over by the London boroughs and the City of London.

MAP SHOWING THE MAIN LOCAL GOVERNMENT DIVISIONS

— county council boundaries

▨ Metropolitan areas

▦ Greater London area

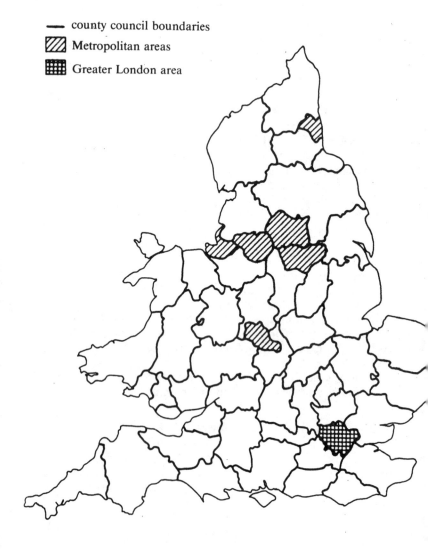

D) JOINT BOARDS

As far as b) and c) are concerned, the metropolitan areas and London, there are also a maze of bodies which have been established since 1986 following abolition of the MCCs and GLC. These are called joint boards, authorities, successor bodies and residuary bodies. Their role and responsibilities will be dealt with fully in section 2.2(d).

E) PARISH, TOWN AND COMMUNITY COUNCILS

In addition to the local authorities already described in this chapter, there are small local councils called parish, town or community councils throughout England and Wales. These councils elect their councillors once every four years and, although they are not a major tier of local government, they do have powers to provide services, comment on planning applications and provide small grants to voluntary organisations (see section 2.2(e) for responsibilities).

2.2 Responsibilities

Local authorities are responsible for a wide range of services which are described below. They also take an overview of the needs of their areas, for example, in relation to housing and industrial development, recreational and arts provision, and the use of land, roads and buildings generally. The division of responsibilities between the authorities is as follows:

A) THE NON-METROPOLITAN AREAS

(i) County councils
- Social services
  (child care, families, people with handicaps, elderly)
- Education
  (Nursery schools, schools, colleges, adult education). The provisions of the Education Reform Act 1988 are dealt with in 2.3(b).
- Libraries
- Environment and planning
  (structure plans, development control, transport planning, county and national parks, gypsy sites, land use (acquisition, disposal and clearance of land), traffic controls, maintenance and renewal of roads and pavements, street lighting,

road safety, development of road networks, public transport, provision of footpaths)
- Public protection
(fire services, consumer protection, weights and measures, emergency services)
- Agriculture (if appropriate)
(small holdings, farming issues)
- Economic/industrial development
- Other general policy responsibilities
(arts, leisure, sports, museums, airports, tourism, equal opportunities (race equality, women and disability), public relations, grants to voluntary bodies, various registration and licensing functions)

The above responsibilities are administered by the major committees of county councils. Responsibilities can be dealt with by different committees, eg in some areas gypsy sites could come under the Policy Committee and libraries could come under the Education Committee. However, in other counties, libraries could be administered by a separate 'Libraries Committee' and gypsy sites could come under the Environment or Planning Committee. If you want to find out which committee is responsible for a particular function listed above, contact the Chief Executive's Office and ask which department/committee deals with that function (see chapter 3 on how departments and committees work).

(ii) District councils
- Housing
(provision and maintenance of council housing; homelessness; improvement and repairs grant) (overall responsibility for provision of social rented housing, homelessness, improvement grants, etc. See section 2.3(c) and chapter 7 - for change in role and provision)
- Planning
(planning applications for individual properties (change of use, extensions and adaptions, district or local plans, conservation and land use), footpaths, gypsy sites, caravan sites and allotments)
- Technical services
(direct labour organisation and public works (council house repairs))

- Leisure/parks and amenities
  (parks, swimming pools, galleries, playgrounds, leisure centres)
  Ground maintenance is now subject to competitive tendering (see section 2.3(a)).
- Environmental health
  (public health, waste disposal, rubbish collection, local sewers, clean air, noise nuisance, markets, cemeteries and crematoria, control of office, shop and factory premises)
  Refuse collection is now subject to competitive tendering.
- Transport
  (district councils used to be public transport operators. Since the de-regulation of bus services in 1986, the district councils' role has been diminished considerably as they are no longer bus operators)
- Other General Policy Functions
  (economic and industrial development, equal opportunities, public relations, tourism, grants to voluntary bodies, arts and entertainments, airports, licensing and registrative functions)

Again you will find that there are different names for some of these major headings, most of which will be the names of the main council committees. Some of the functions will be dealt with by sub-committees of a general policy committee, eg land, licensing, industrial/economic development. In some rural areas, there may be two major functions joined into one department, for example, housing and environmental health are often brought together under one chief officer.

B) METROPOLITAN AREAS

(i) Metropolitan districts
These councils are responsible for:
- Social services
- Education (see 2.3(b))
- Libraries
- Housing (see 2.3(c))
- Planning and control of building
- Technical services
- Leisure/parks and amenities
- Environmental health
- Consumer protection
- Other General Policy Functions of district councils.

(see section 2.2(a)(i) and (ii) for fuller explanations of these responsibilities)
There are arrangements for carrying out other responsibilities of local government since the abolition of MCCs which will be dealt with under section 2.2(d).

C) THE LONDON BOROUGHS

(i) The functions of the *London boroughs*, both 'inner' and 'outer' are as follows:
- Libraries
- Housing
- Local traffic
- Leisure/parks and amenities
- Planning and control of building
- Environmental health (including refuse collection)

(For changes arising as a result of new legislation in housing, leisure and amenities, and environmental health, see section 2.3.)
- Consumer protection
- Other General Policy Functions (see section 2.2 (a) (i) and (ii) for further explanations of these responsibilities).

The 'outer' London boroughs also have responsibility for education.
(ii)   As mentioned above, the ILEA was abolished in April 1990 with the London boroughs and the City of London taking on the education functions of the ILEA.

D) JOINT BOARDS
Since abolition of the GLC and MCCs, various joint boards and authorities have taken on the responsibilities of the abolished councils.

(i) Co-ordinating committees
These have been established in each of the seven areas affected by abolition (London and the Metropolitan areas). They include one councillor from each of the borough and district councils in each area. These committees were set up to help transfer the functions of the abolished councils to the metropolitan districts. They can establish other committees and bodies to take responsibility for certain functions. For example, the London Co-ordinating Committee was responsible for set-

ting up the *London Borough Grants Scheme* (see Appendix 1). This scheme co-ordinates the funding of voluntary organisations whose work crosses more than one London borough, or provides services London-wide (see section 8.4(i)).

(ii) Residuary bodies
These have been set up by the government under the Local Government Act 1985 to deal with various outstanding matters arising from the abolished councils, eg – disposing of the property of the councils, managing pension funds, dealing with former staff who have not been appropriately re-employed. There is one body for each of the seven areas, with up to 10 members appointed by the government. Some of the residuary bodies have been wound up. However, in London the residuary body is being used to deal with the abolition of the ILEA.

(iii) Joint authorities/boards
In each of the seven areas there are joint boards (also called authorities) which have been set up to deal with the following responsibilities:
- Police
- Fire and civil defence
- Passenger transport
- Waste disposal (in some areas)

As far as waste disposal is concerned, in some areas arrangements have been made between districts to deal with waste disposal. In other areas, statutory joint authorities have been set up. (Waste disposal is concerned with how and where to get rid of rubbish. Waste regulation deals with the licensing of sites and the transportation of hazardous waste.)

In London the Passenger Transport Authority is called *London Regional Transport*, responsible for London's buses and the Underground.

(iv) Inter-borough successor authorities
In London some boroughs have set up inter-borough authorities to deal with some of the London-wide policies and services which the GLC was formerly responsible for.

There are other 'successor authorities' with elected members involved, but not all boroughs belong, such as the *London Boroughs Disability Resource Team, the London Housing Unit, the London Area Mobility Scheme-Joint Committee* and many more.

There are also other successor bodies which do not have elected members on them but are directly appointed by government. These include the joint boards already mentioned. They also include some existing quangos (bodies set up and appointed by government) such as the *Arts Council* which can give grants to arts organisations, the *Sports Council*, the *London Planning Commission* and many others.

(v) Other responsibilities not covered by joint boards or authorities
There are other responsibilities of the abolished MCCs and GLCs which have not been listed here. These may be dealt with jointly by the metropolitan districts or London boroughs in one of their joint committees or they may dealt with by one council acting for all the others in the area.

For further detailed information about the situation in London, consult *Who's Who in London Government* published by the *London Voluntary Services Council* (see Appendix 1) or the *London Government Directory* published by the *Association of London Authorities* (see Appendix 1). For London and the metropolitan areas, information can be obtained from the residuary bodies, joint co-ordinating committees and the *Association of Metropolitan Authorities* (see chapter 12 and Appendix 1).

E) PARISH, TOWN AND COMMUNITY COUNCILS
These councils can develop, provide and influence many local services, some of which they will deal with in conjunction with another organisation or local authority. They have powers in relation to the following services:
- Allotments
- Arts
- Baths and swimming pools
- Cemeteries and mortuaries
- Churchyards
- Clocks
- Commons, open spaces and village greens
- Entertainments
- Halls
- Lighting
- Litter
- Parking places
- Playing fields
- Public lavatories

- Roadside verges
- Seats, shelters and signs
- Tourism

Parish, town and community councils can also give grants to voluntary bodies.

For further information about town councils see *Powers and Constitution of Local Councils,* published by the *National Association of Local Councils* (see Appendix 1).

F) THE POLICE

(i) Non-metropolitan areas

The police are not directly accountable to local authorities. In England and Wales the Police Authorities are either committees of the county councils or they are 'combined Police Authorities' bringing together several county council areas.

Those which are Committees of the Council can be questioned by council members about their policies, duties and actions. The Police Committees will draw up their own budgets and they have to be approved by the local authority, as do their standing orders. There is, however, usually little opportunity for the local authorities to change or amend the police budgets, even though they are meeting part of the costs of the police operations in their areas.

The same situation applies to the combined Police Authorities where several county councils are brought together and contribute to the budget of the Police Authority. The constituent councils have no power to question or reject the budget, and they can present the councils with a bill for their part of the costs regardless of the local authorities' views on the merits and size of the budget.

Membership of the Police Committees and Authorities is drawn from the constituent councils and from magistrates appointed by the local magistrates committees (one-third of the membership are magistrates).

(ii) Metropolitan areas

In the metropolitan areas joint boards have been set up following abolition, with membership drawn from councillors in the constituent metropolitan district councils and one-third drawn from magistates (see 2.2d(iii)). Representatives from local authorities must be in proportion to the political party representation in each council.

(iii) London
The Metropolitan Police force is not accountable to any locally elected police authority. It is directly accountable to the Home Secretary. In addition, the City of London Corporation has its own police force.

(iv) Initiatives to introduce local monitoring of Police Authorities
Some local authorities have established their own internal Police Committees to provide support to their members on the Police Authorities, to examine agendas, reports, and ensure that they are informed and briefed before Police Authority meetings so that they can contribute fully to the discussions. Police activity in the local authority's area is often monitored by these internal committees. Contact your local authority to see if they have a Police Committee. Make sure you are clear about the differences between these Committees and the Police Authorities themselves. They are often called police monitoring or support units.

G) THE PROBATION SERVICE
The probation service is managed by locally established Probation Committees which in the shire counties consist of magistrates and a small number of co-opted members who are appointed by the committees. In the metropolitan and London areas, elected members from the local authorities sit on the local Probation Committees, together with magistrates and other co-opted members. 20 per cent of the costs of the local probation service is funded by the county councils, metopolitan districts and London boroughs with the remaining 80 per cent financed by the Home Office.

2.3 Recent changes in local authority service provision
As has been indicated in this chapter, the changes in law since 1987 have had a major effect on our council services. These are described below in greater detail.

A) COMPETITIVE TENDERING UNDER THE LOCAL GOVERNMENT ACT 1988
Under this Act the following areas of council work will have to

be put out to competitive tender, if the local authority wishes to provide them 'in-house':

- Refuse collection
- Cleaning of schools and other buildings
- Other cleaning, eg street cleaning, litter bins
- Catering - school and welfare
- All other catering (eg in council buildings)
- Ground maintenance (parks etc)
- Vehicle repair and maintenance
- Sports and Leisure management (this was added later by the Secretary of State)

The timetable lays down that the tendering must take place between 1989 and 1991 with differing contract periods.

These changes are important to understand for the consumer who may find that some of their essential council services are run by private companies. Local authorities will be able to tender themselves for the contract, but they can only award themselves the contract if their bid is the lowest or if they can show some other good reason for doing so. They will be closely scrutinised by commercial bidders and the Secretary of State.

The Act has major implications for voluntary organisations receiving grants from local authorities for work they are doing in these areas and for those who may be contemplating becoming involved in these areas of work, eg catering (meals on wheels), waste-recycling projects, some energy conservation projects, environmental projects involved in parks and voluntary projects in leisure management. Up to now these grants were awarded for the work done as a matter of policy in an uncompetitive situation. Now the local authority may have to put out to tender the work which your organisation has been involved in doing, particularly if your organisation has a contract to undertake the work and has a council representative on its management committee. (See also chapter 8, Sources of finance for voluntary organisations from local authorities.)

Other issues of concern relate to the restrictions placed on local authorities in vetting potential contracts for equal opportunities policies and practice as contracts can only be awarded on commercial grounds. The only exceptions to this relate to statutory provisions under the Race Relations Act 1976 and the requirements for disability quotas. However, a council does have to be satisfied that the contract or their own direct service organisation (DSO) meets nationally agreed service standards, is responsive to users and consults with users about the service. These would be the areas where the consumer could make representations about the quality and availability of service.

B) EDUCATION REFORM ACT 1988

As mentioned above, the Education Act introduced changes which reduce the control of the local education authority over the running of schools. Under the Local Management of Schools (LMS) arrangements, the financial management of all secondary schools and primary schools with more than 200 pupils is being delegated to the governing bodies who will have to plan and organise how to use the budgetary allocation which they will receive from the local authority to cover all the basic running costs of the school. The local education authority (LEA) will generally retain direct responsibility for some matters such as the structural aspects of the school buildings and various centrally provided services, depending how the local scheme for financial management has been drawn up. The make-up of governing bodies has changed since September 1988 with the inclusion of more parent governors elected by the parents of the school, precise provision for co-opted governors (including the requirement to ensure the adequate representation of the local business community) and fewer LEA nominees.

In addition to this, the Act includes a provision for all secondary schools and primary schools with over 300 pupils to 'opt out' of local authority control from September 1989 and become 'grant maintained' by the Department of Education ad Science (DES). The parents of a school can seek to have a (secret) ballot held if they have the support of 20 per cent of the parent body. A second ballot must be held if under 50 per cent of all parents in the school do not take part in the ballot. The result of the second ballot is binding on the governors regardless of how many voted. The Secretary of State can refuse to allow an 'opt out' to take place if there is not a clear show of support from the parents. If the school does 'opt out' there will be a new governing body set up which will be responsible for all the school's finances and which will receive a grant directly from central government instead of support from the local education authority which will in turn lose a proportion of its government grant to compensate.

Other issues affecting parents include the introduction of

'open enrolment', which means that a LEA will generally not be able to enforce catchment areas, except perhaps where a school has reached its physical capacity. The change has been introduced in the expectation that it should give parents greater effective choice as to which school their child attends although the practical options will vary.

The Act requires local education authorities to draw up a plan for further and higher education provision in their areas. This must make clear a set of objectives and in drawing up a plan, the LEA must consult other bodies contributing to further and higher education. This could include voluntary organisations providing training and educational courses for adults such as the Workers Educational Association and Womens/ Youth/Community Skills Training Workshops.

C) HOUSING ACT 1988

Under the Housing Act 1988 private landlords and housing associations 'approved' by the Housing Corporation (Tai Cymru in Wales) can bid to buy up council houses, taking over as a new landlord following a ballot of the tenants. Council tenants can also approach a new 'approved landlord' to take over their homes under the Tenants' Choice procedures or they could form themselves into a 'tenant-owned' body which could apply for approval from the Housing Corporation or Tai Cymru to become a landlord and pursue the Tenants' Choice procedures. As has been said, in any of these situations a ballot has to be held of tenants about the proposal, and 50 per cent of the tenants affected must vote in the ballot for it to be valid. However, those tenants who do not vote will be counted as voting in favour of the proposal. Only those who voted against the transfer to a new landlord will be able to stay as council tenants. A local authority cannot stop the Tenants' Choice procedures from being initiated whether by tenants' or landlords.

There are various stages and procedures leading up to the formal ballot of tenants if Tenants' Choice is being used. Tenants in this situation at the time of writing have sought independent advice and information to help them understand the procedures and implications of Tenants' Choice. TPAS (Tenant Participation Advisory Service) has produced information for tenants about the scheme including a tenants' guide to tenants choice (see Appendix for addresses and details of publications). See also *The Housing Act 1988* published by Shelter.

The Act also makes provision for a council to transfer all or part of its stock to an 'approved landlord' so that it is no longer the main or sole 'provider' of social/public rented housing in their district. This option is being considered by several local authorities at the time of writing with some voluntary transfers going through, eg Sevenoaks. The procedures for promoting a voluntary transfer are not as clear as those for Tenants' Choice, and approval for the transfer has to be gained from the Department of Environment or Welsh Office, not the Housing Corporation or Tai Cymru. For example, there is no statutory requirement for a new landlord to hold a ballot. However, it is unlikely that a transfer would be approved unless tenants had been consulted in this way. At the time of writing organisations like TPAS are drawing up guidelines for tenants and local authorities as to how tenants should be consulted and what safeguards should be given to enable them to make an informed choice. Again, of crucial importance is the need to make independent information and advice available for tenants with such a major change being proposed which affects not only the ownership of their homes, but their rights as tenants. The government has not provided resources for tenants to seek this advice although some local authorities have seen the need to consult their tenants if they wish to pursue the voluntary transfer successfully.

D) LOCAL GOVERNMENT AND HOUSING ACT 1989

Under this Act there are major changes to local government finance which are dealt with in chapter 7, and also changes which affect political control and relationships between voluntary organisations and local authorities which are dealt with in chapters 3 and 5. There are also new economic development and advice powers given to local authorities which may assist in the funding of voluntary organisations (see chapter 8). However, as far as functions of local authorities are concerned, a major change is the introduction of means testing of improvement grants. Owner occupiers must now have their income, savings and ability to borrow money assessed by the local authority in considering whether to give grant approval, and landlords must be assessed to see if they are able to recover repair and improvement costs through rental income. Means testing of people with disabilities who apply for grants and adaptations now takes place, and the only new benefit is a minor grant for elderly people to insulate their homes or their relatives' homes if it enables them to stay living in the community. These are only available to people whose incomes are below a certain level.

There are also provisions in this Act to enable local councils to introduce charges for any services with only a few exceptions (eg education, police, fire service, elections and borrowing books for libraries). The Secretary of State can require charges to be introduced for public library services (other than book borrowing) and can state what level and type of charges can be introduced (see chapter 7).

3

How Local Government Works

This chapter will explain how local government works in terms of the structure and responsibilities of council departments, including those which provide a service to the public and those which carry out the administrative functions of the council. It will deal with the way in which council committees are organised, their membership, and the role played by the officers of the local authority at council meetings. It will look at the role of the chairs of committees. The technicalities of how decisions are made by committees will be discussed, such as the use of 'delegated powers', as well as how long it will take for committee decisions to be implemented, how emergency decisions can be taken and whether council decisions can be reconsidered. It will explain the position of mayor/chair of the council, and it will explain your rights to information about council meetings and proceedings.

3.1 Councillors, chief officers, departments and committees

Local authorities are organised into a number of departments with all major decisions being made by committees of councillors. Councillors are elected representatives who are commonly referred to as members of the authority. Elections take place every four years. In some councils, elections take place in three out of four years with a proportion of councillors standing for re-election, if they have served four years. District council elections are held at different times from county council elections, eg the most recent county council elections were held in May 1989, while most district council elections will be held in May 1991.

POLITICALLY RESTRICTED POSTS
The Local Government and Housing Act 1989 has introduced restrictions on who may stand for election as a councillor. This has been referred to as 'twin tracking'. The following people are disqualified from standing for election:
- a chief executive, chief officers or deputies
- a monitoring officer (see 3.1(a))
- political advisers to party groups
- those earning at least £19,500 and who speak on behalf of the local authority

There will be an appeals procedures for any staff who consider that their posts have been wrongly designated as 'politically restricted'.

The Act also introduced a provision for the Secretary of State to have a code of practice for local councillors known as the National Code of Local Government Conduct. There has to be consultation with local government representatives on the Code and it has to be approved by Parliament before it is issued. The undertaking to accept this 'Code' may be included in the declaration councillors have to make when they accept office after being elected.

Officers are the paid local government officials who run the authority on a day-to-day basis. In addition to restricting councillors in their ability to work for a local authority, officers obviously face the same restrictions the other way round, preventing them from seeking political office if they hold 'politically restricted posts' (see 3.1 above). If you are a council officer in one of these posts you will not be able to stand as a councillor, MP or MEP. Further restrictions on your out of hours 'political activity and freedom of speech' may be introduced in regulations not published at the time of writing. These may include restrictions on your right to speak or write publicly on political matters. You may also be restricted from canvassing at elections and from holding any positions in political parties. (See LGIU Briefing Notes – Appendix for address.)

Most local authorities will have a chief executive who is the chief officer in overall charge of the council and its departments. Under the Local Government and Housing Act 1989, the chief executive has got an enhanced role. The Act specifies that there must be a chief officer 'as head of their paid service' who is likely to be the chief executive and he or she may determine what resources they need to carry out their duties. In addition, the Act introduces the role of a 'monitoring officer' whose job it is to check that the council is not breaking the law, or offending any code of practice or operating in a way which would not be upheld by the Local Government Ombudsman (see chapter 9). The chief executive could act as the monitoring officer but not as the chief financial officer (treasurer) as well. The monitoring officer role cannot be taken by the chief financial officer. However, the chief executive can act as the chief financial officer if he or she does not take on the monitoring role.

Each department will have a chief officer who will be responsible for implementing the policies of the department, and he or she will generally sit on a management team with the chief executive to ensure effective liaison and communication between departments and to consider strategies for the local authority as a whole. In some smaller authorities, a chief officer may be responsible for more than one department, for example, linking housing and environmental health. Also, the chief executive's role may be combined with the chief officer of another department, eg finance or legal, but as has been said, the monitoring role cannot be combined with the financial role at chief officer level.

The departments can be divided into service departments whose function it is to deliver a service directly to the public (such as housing or social services) and administrative or co-ordinating departments. Among these departments are:

A) CHIEF EXECUTIVE'S OR TOWN CLERK'S DEPARTMENT

As has been described, most councils, whether district or county, will have a chief executive's department (sometimes known as the town clerk's department), and many councils will have other high-ranking administrative officers in the chief executive's department (known as county or borough secretaries or chief administrators) who will be responsible to the chief executive for the administration of the council and the implementation of local authorities' policies. The department will provide clerks to the committees which decide the policies. The clerks will 'service' the committees, preparing agendas and producing the minutes, following up committee decisions with the relevant council departments concerned. For example, the social services committee will have a committee clerk from the chief executive's department who will liaise with the director of social services in the planning of agendas, organisation of meetings and follow up of administrative action that needs to be taken.

The chief executive's department may also be responsible for such areas of work as public relations and equal opportunities. Race relations, women and disability units are often located in these departments if they do not form separate departments of their own. Other major policy functions may also be the responsibility of the chief executive's department such as industrial and economic development, grants to voluntary bodies, arts, welfare rights, police, 'decentralisation' initiatives, and tourism. If you are dealing with any of these functions it is important to ask whether they have their own departments or are dealt with as units of the chief executive's department.

B) TREASURER'S DEPARTMENT
Every local authority will have a Treasurer's Department with a treasurer as the chief officer responsible for all financial transactions controlling the spending of the authority according to the policies agreed by the council. Overall policy about the budget and spending a council can carry out is usually overseen by the finance committee of the authority. This can be a 'free standing' committee (a committee that has powers to make decisions without being referred to another committee for approval (see 3.2(a)) or a sub-committee of the main policy committee of the council. In some councils, financial responsibility can be incorporated into a policy and resources committee which agrees the annual budget, oversees its spending and takes responsibility for agreeing the overall policy objectives of the council.

C) PERSONNEL DEPARTMENT

Every local authority will have a personnel manager and department responsible for the pay and conditions of the staff of the local authority. There will be a personnel committee which will deal with all staff matters, including trade union representation on general staffing matters, and particular issues such as equal opportunity policies and training. It will also have machinery to deal with disputes and disciplinary matters.

D) LEGAL DEPARTMENT

All councils will have a legal department with a solicitor as the chief officer responsible for all legal transactions and interpretations of legislation affecting the different departments of the council. They are also responsible for ensuring that the local authority is acting within the law (see 3.1(e) below). A representative from the solicitor's legal department will often attend committee meetings to advise councillors on the laws relating to policies they are discussing and the interpretation of standing orders.

E) SERVICE DEPARTMENTS

In chapter 2, the main responsibilities of the departments which provide a service to the public were outlined – such as housing, social servies, education, environmental health, traffic orders, etc. These departments will be responsible for their own policies and budgets as agreed by their committees and by the overall budget and policies of the council. If a service department wanted to adopt a policy which required an increase in spending during the year over and above their allocated amount, or if they wanted to adopt a radically new policy which would affect other departments of the council, then these matters would be brought to the main policy committee of the council for consideration. Otherwise each service committee will to a large extent run their own affairs. The service committees will often require advice and information from the various administrative and co-ordinating departments just mentioned. For example, if a social services committee were considering refusing the registration of a private home for the elderly, the legal department would advise the committee as to whether they had adequate legal grounds to do so.

3.2 How a committee works

A) THE STATUS OF COMMITTEES

Councils are governed by a system of committees of councillors. As has been explained, there will generally be a committee for each service department and an overall policy committee which deals with wider issues of spending plans, limits and policy matters. There will also be some internal committees which may be sub-committees of the policy committee, such as the personnel committee described in 3.1. If they are not sub-committees, these committees are called 'standing' or 'free standing' committees of the council. This means that they are the major committees of the council to which the chief officers report, and they will be responsible for their departments' policies and services. Section 3.3 deals with the cycles of council meetings, explaining the route a decision takes from consideration at a committee to full approval by the whole council.

Committees can set up sub-committees or working parties of councillors to deal with specialised aspects of policy; for example, a housing committee would generally have a housing allocations/tenancy sub-committee which would deal with the allocation of tenancies. In some circumstances sub-committees can have the power to make decisions without them being referred to the main 'standing' committee for discussion. In these circumstances they have 'delegated powers' (see 3.7). However, most sub-committees would make recommendations to the main committees for them to consider. The major service departments will do most of their business through sub-committees which deal with the nuts and bolts of policy developments and expenditure plans.

In addition to sub-committees, some committees will have 'advisory committees' and/or working parties whose brief it is to advise the local authority through the policy committee on a particular piece of policy affecting all departments. Advisory committees can only make recommendations on policy, to the major 'standing' or 'full' committees as they are sometimes called.

B) COUNCIL MEMBERSHIP OF COMMITTEES

Councillors will be appointed to various committees. The sizes and numbers of committees will be decided prior to the Annual

AN EXAMPLE OF ONE SOCIAL SERVICES COMMITTEE'S SUB-COMMITTEES

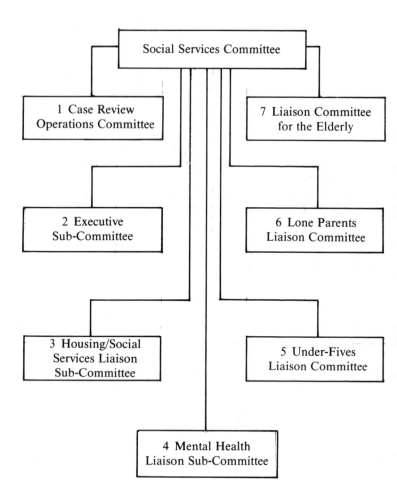

General Meeting. (New committees can be set up during the year if approved by the full council.) The party group 'in control' of the council (see chapter 4) will decide what committees it wants, the size, etc., but since the Local Government and Housing Act 1989 was introduced, the places on the committees have to be taken up in proportion to the number of seats won by each party at the elections (see 4.1(a)). The only exception to this relates to area/neighbourhood committees which cover less than a third of the local authority's area. These committees would not be required to meet the party political balance provided on central council committees.

The size, composition and membership of the committees will be decided at the Annual Meetings, so it is important to check when your council holds these meetings to maintain an up-to-date list of committee members. Major changes are only likely to take place after elections. However, some councillors may decide to move off a committee and be replaced during the year, so always check that there have been no changes with the chief executive's department.

As each committee will be served by a clerk from the chief executive's department, advised by the officers from the department to which the committee is attached and other officers, eg, legal, financial or personnel, you will often find a great many people in attendance at a council committee meeting who are not the elected councillors.

C) CO-OPTED MEMBERS

Many councils have committees where they have co-opted people from outside the council who have particular experience, or represent users of the service or represent minorities or groups who are under-represented in the council membership. For example, many committees concerned with race and women's equality co-opt from outside, also people with disabilities are often co-opted onto various committees to be given a voice. In some cases there may be a joint committee with an outside body such as a Council for Racial Equality. Council tenants are co-opted on to housing committees in some councils, and other councils have set up local 'area committees' or neighbourhood forums involving tenants, residents and minority groups not represented on the committee.

This has all been affected by the Local Government and Housing Act 1989 which rules that co-opted members cannot vote on council committees. The right to vote has been of major importance to many of these groups who are poorly represented on local authorities. The co-opted members have been nominated or elected by their own groups and constituencies to put forward and represent their views, so widening the accountability of local government. The new Act still allows for co-options but without voting rights. However, co-optees on advisory committees, consultative committees and working parties will still have the right to vote as these committees are not 'decision making', they only advise or put forward recommendations to a committee which has the power to make policy and take decisions. If councils are committed to giving the co-optees the right to influence and make policy, they will have to ensure that the recommendations and advice coming from these advisory committees are backed when they reach a formal committee of councillors. It is also important that co-opted members have full access to committee papers, speaking rights and the ability to ask for information from officers and councillors.

The Act allows for non-council members to vote on local management committees of council facilities, eg community centres. It also will allow for tenants to vote on estate management boards/committees which have been set up to manage a specific estate or part of an estate. This exemption will be given if they are discharging this management function under sections 20–26 of the Housing Act 1985. However, the exemption will only be given if the number of houses on the estate (or part of an estate) does not exceed one-sixth of the council's total housing stock. As far as area or neighbourhood committees are concerned (often set up as part of a de-centralisation policy), co-opted members cannot vote.

D) OBSERVER STATUS

Local authorities can also have people with 'observer status' on their committees. This status is granted to members of the local authorities, outside organisations and individuals. Under its terms, a person can contribute to the committee proceedings, receive notices of meetings and agendas, speak, but not vote.

3.3 Cycles of meetings

Local authorities transact business in 'cycles' of meetings. In a cycle, each of the main committees will normally meet once. Sub-committees of the main committees may meet once in a cycle or more infrequently depending on the amount of business the sub-committee incurs and the length of the cycles. At the end of the cycle the whole council will meet to consider the minutes of all the committee meetings held during that cycle. This is usually referred to as the 'full council'. This 'full council' meeting has the final say and it is only when it has approved the minutes of the committees that the decisions within them can be implemented unless delegated powers have been given to the committees (see 3.7). If, for example, you have heard that a committee has approved a grant application from your organisation it may not be awarded until it has been passed by the 'full council'.

The length of these cycles of meetings varies from one authority to another, from four weeks to eight weeks or longer in some rural authorities. The council will usually present a timetable of committee and council meetings for the year to the Annual General Meeting. The 'cycles' will usually take into account a break for a month in the summer (August) so you will find there is a long gap between an early summer council meeting and an autumn meeting. Additional meetings may be held during particularly busy periods of the council's year, such as budget-making time, from October to February.

3.4 How to get hold of council agendas, summons and minutes

As has been said there will be a timetable of meetings drawn up at least a year in advance, and you can ask for information from the chief executive's department about when a particular committee is meeting.

Agendas for committee meetings are sent out to councillors prior to the meetings and since the Local Government (Access to Information) Act 1985 was passed, the public has the right to inspect and copy the agenda of any council, committee, or sub-committee meeting three days before the meeting takes place. A notice should be put up in the main council offices at least three days before a council meeting is held informing the public of the time date and place of the meeting.

Since the Access to Information Act, you should be able to see not only the agendas of meetings but also any reports and background papers which are being submitted to the committee, such as background information for the agenda items and reports.

The agenda for the 'full council' meeting is generally referred to as the 'summons', and it will include all the minutes of all the committees and sub-committees held during the cycle. This is a most useful record to keep in order to check up and refer to decisions made by the council. This summons is the public record of the council's decisions and copies should be available in the public library. Also, under the Access to Information Act you should be able to obtain your own copy of the summons three days in advance of the full council meeting and acquire one at the meeting itself.

Each committee will have its own recorded minutes which are available to the public under the new Act. However, if part of the committee was held in private because of 'exempt information' (see section 3.5 below), only a summary will be given of the proceedings of that part of the meeting. Obviously you may need to inspect the minutes as soon as possible after the committee meeting has been held, but if you are not in a hurry it is usually most convenient to inspect them when the summons has been drawn up for the full council meeting as the committee minutes are all published together in one book. Again, if you do obtain a copy of a sub-committee's minutes recording a decision in your favour don't forget that the decision is likely to be subject to the approval of the main committee and the full council.

3.5 The public's right to information about council business

The Local Government (Access to Information) Act 1985 has given the public many more rights to find out about forthcoming and past council business. However, the Community Rights Project, which has done a great deal of work in campaigning for this Act and monitoring its implementation, has found that some councils have not always fulfilled their obligations (see Appendix 1). You might find that a council official is not very helpful or forthcoming when you make an approach for information, but your rights to information are clearly laid down in the Act. If you find that the council is not complying with the

Act you can report them to your local councillor, the ombudsman/woman, the police, or tell the press or the Community Rights Project, or your local council for voluntary service (CVS). As has been explained in section 3.4, the new Act allows you to:

(i)   inspect or copy the agendas of committees or council meeting three days before a meeting

(ii) see the background papers used in the preparation of reports presented to the committee and the information reports presented to the committee members

(iii) inspect the minutes of meetings except for parts of the meetings where 'exempt information' (see below) is involved. However, you are entitled to a summary of those discussions.

You may have to pay a small charge for photocopying documents you want copies of, but you should be able to get reports, agendas and minutes of meetings free. Unfortunately, some local authorities impose excessive charges.

'Exempt Information' includes information relating to employees, office-holders, applicants for jobs within the council; tenants, applicants for tenancies; recipients of services; individuals receiving financial assistance; consideration of fostering, adoption, child care cases; matters relating to particular contracts and tenders and any action taken in connection with a crime that is being investigated or prosecuted.

OTHER RIGHTS UNDER THE ACT

(i)   The Act has also enabled you to request the names and addresses of councillors and the committees they are serving on.

(ii) Agendas and reports should be open to you for up to six years and internal documents are open to you for four years.

(iii) You should be able to find out if an officer of the authority has got the right to take decisions on behalf of the council and you can find out exactly what his or her duties or powers are (eg during holiday periods or emergencies (see 3.8)).

For further information about the Act see the *Wallchart on the Access to Information Act* and the *Guide to Councillors' Rights to Information* published by the *Community Rights Project* (full details in Appendix 1).

3.6 Standing orders

It is useful to obtain a copy of your council's standing orders because they will explain the rules by which the council operates its committees, when it uses delegated powers, how it takes emergency decisions, etc. Standing orders can change, so make sure you check up on them regularly.

Under the new Local Government and Housing Act 1989 the Secretary of State has the power to insist that standing orders are introduced which all councils must follow.

3.7 Delegated powers of committees

In section 3.2(a) we mentioned the fact that some committees and sub-committees have 'delegated powers'. This means that they can take a decision which does not have to be approved by any other committee of the council.

Individual councils will make their own decisions as to which committees and under what circumstances they will be given delegated powers. A council can delegate any power to a committee except the power to raise a rate or borrow money.

If delegated powers apply, a councillor cannot seek to 'amend' or 'refer back' or vote against a decision which has been agreed under delegated powers unless the council decides to suspend its standing orders, but the councillor can write to the chief executive and ask for the matter to be reconsidered by the committee concerned (see section 3.9 below).

These 'delegated' powers vary from authority to authority. Some councils do a great deal of business through delegated powers. Others will try to limit them to enable wider discussion of recommendations rather than leave it to the consideration of one group of councillors on a committee. If you want to find out when your local council uses 'delegated powers', ask for a copy of their 'standing orders' which will identify the functions of committees and their powers. (Examples of where delegated powers are sometimes used: traffic orders; planning applications; housing allocations.)

3.8 Emergency powers

Local authorities can also make decisions through using 'emergency powers' outlined in their standing orders. This might involve the leader of the council and/or the chairs of the committee or party spokesmen or women in making a decision in 'an emergency' outside a committee meeting, acting with the advice of the chief executive and chief officers. An emergency decision cannot be made by one councillor alone. The Access to Information Act requires councils to inform the public of their decision-making process, including how they make emergency decisions. Therefore councils may use the power that can be delegated to a council officer, under the Act, such as the chief executive, to enable him or her to make decisions in an emergency. But the chief executive would only take such steps if he could not call a special meeting of leading councillors involved to take an emergency decision. If decisions have been made using 'emergency powers' they should be reported to the next meeting of the appropriate committee. Again, your council's standing orders will explain how decisions are taken in an emergency.

3.9 Reconsidering decisions

If a decision has been approved by a committee and by the full council there will often be a standing order of the council which specifies that the decision cannot be re-considered for a certain period of time, eg six months. For example, if the council adopts a recommendation to declare their area a 'nuclear free zone', this decision cannot be reversed for the specified period of time. Most councils will have standing orders which do enable councillors to ask for matters to be reconsidered by a committee, or councillors can propose a motion about a decision which had previously been rejected before the time period is up. This usually has to be signed by a number of councillors (eg a third). If you want to find out the procedures for reversing or reconsidering decisions, ask your chief executive for a copy of the council's standing orders.

3.10 Officers' role at committee meetings

As has already been explained, the paid officials of a council are not members of the council committees – their role is to prepare the agenda papers and reports for the committees and to advise them. The final decisions rest with the councillors (see 5.5).

3.11 Chairs of committees – who are they? What is their role?

Each committee is chaired by a councillor and there is one (or sometimes more) vice-chair. These chairs are important in the decision-making process. They are elected annually by the committees following the Annual General Meetings. If there is a party political group in power they are usually nominated and supported by the controlling group (see 4.1(b)). If there is a 'hung' council or a council which is not controlled by one political party, each party may 'take turns' annually or for each 'cycle' to chair a committee, or there may be an agreed system of nominating chairs based on such factors as seniority (see 4.1(h) and 4.1(i)). Alternatively, the party with the greatest number of seats in the council may take the chairs with the support of other parties.

3.12 The mayor/chair of the council

Most district authorities will have a mayoral position, held by a councillor, who will also act as the chair of full council meetings during his/her year of office. The mayors are usually chosen according to seniority and length of service and they may alternate between the political parties. The mayor can be from a political party which is not 'in control' of the council. However, some councils pick the mayor from the political party 'in control' of the council. He or she does not usually have a political role to play, but will be the 'ambassador' for the council during that year. County councils do not have mayors but will have a similar post known as the chair of the council, responsible for chairing full council meetings and again playing a non-political ambassadorial role with the same procedures for selection as with mayors. (These positions are not to be confused with 'leaders' of the council (see section 4.1(c)).

The role of the chair in 'hung' authorities (see 4.1(h)) is somewhat different. It can be used 'politically', because the full council meetings tend to become involved in major decisions, such as agreeing the budget, and so the chair might be called upon to use a casting vote in a hung situation, thereby exerting a major influence on the policies of the council.

4
How Decisions Are Made - The 'Power Structure'

This chapter will look at the effect of the party political control on councils, explaining what is meant by the party 'in control', the 'group', the 'whip', the 'leader', etc. It will deal with the situation in 'hung councils'. It will go on to look at the ways in which policies are evolved, leading up to a decision made by a committee, and will look at the influence of officers of the council, councillors, the chairs, and the controlling group. It will deal with committee procedures in relation to 'public consultation' and will consider different ways councils do/do not involve interested people outside the committees in making decisions, for example, formal and informal public consultation, the use of co-optees, working parties, etc.

As with most organisations, the way decisions are actually made by local authorities is as much dictated by discussions behind the scenes as it is by the formal process of a committee's deliberations. Each council will have its own way of working, and within each council the different departments may have quite individual styles in the way they handle business.

In some cases, a committee may discuss an item without there being a preconceived view about it. Sometimes the decision will have been made long before the matter was placed on any committee agenda (see chapter 5). In some cases, the view of the officers of the council will be all-important, sometimes individual councillors will dominate decision-making. It is very difficult to generalise, and familiarity with your own authorities will be the only satisfactory way of finding out how decisions are made. However, there are some pointers which can be helpful and this section will look at them.

The Local Government and Housing Act 1989 introduces a variety of measures which affect party political control in local government and the rights of co-optees. These changes will also be dealt with in this section.

4.1 Political control and party groups

A) COUNCILS WHERE ONE PARTY HAS OVERALL CONTROL

It is important to be aware whether the council is controlled by one political party. A party 'takes control' if it wins a majority of seats on the council at an election and 'forms an administration'. Most councils in urban England and Wales are controlled in this way.

When a party is 'in control', it will usually hold all important positions (such as the chairs of all committees). Under the new Local Government and Housing Act 1989, councillors from all the political parties represented on the council must be appointed to committees in the same proportion to the number of seats they won at the election. (Before the Act, the party that won the majority of seats usually took the majority of places on committees.) This proportional representation also applies to places on outside bodies (see chapter 5).

By controlling the chairs of the committees, and by virtue of their strength in numbers on the committees, the party 'in control' can still exercise considerable power unless it is in a very small minority. To back up the power it can wield, it will have its own machinery to organise how it operates and makes decisions. This machinery is very important, with the central focus of decision-making being vested in the party political groups.

B) THE 'GROUP' – WHAT IS IT?

The councillors on any local authority belonging to a particular party will normally form themselves into a group, known as the 'labour group', the 'conservative group', etc. These groups meet regularly to discuss their views on decisions being made by the council and on its policies. If there is one political group 'in control' of the council this group will in effect plan the basic policies and strategies which the council will follow. The minority groups discuss how to oppose the controlling group and how to promote their own plans and policies. The important point is that these discussions take place in private and the majority group in control will often make major decisions in this way before the issue is discussed in public by a council committee, to ensure they are working within the framework of their party and group policies.

C) THE LEADER OF THE COUNCIL – WHO IS SHE/ HE?

A group on a council normally elects one of its members to chair the group meetings and to lead the group in council debates and discussions. Where a group is in a majority on the council, the leader of that group is known as the leader of the council and generally chairs the policy committee of the council. The leader is the most powerful single member of the council and usually has an office in the council headquarters. She/he will work closely with the chief executive in ensuring that the policies of the council are being implemented. They will be involved in many meetings to discuss policy ideas and to deal with issues arising on a day-to-day basis which need some reponse. The leader will also be involved in meetings with out-side bodies and other authorities.

Many leaders are virtually full-time and will be paid special allowances for loss of earnings.

It is often worthwhile approaching the leader's office and asking for a meeting with them to discuss an issue, problem or to explore the possibilities of obtaining a grant. You could also invite the leader to address a meeting or chair a conference on an issue relevant to the local authority she/he is leading.

The role and power of the leader of a political group in a 'hung council' will be very different from this, as there will not be a 'leader of the council' in the same way as there is in a majority party controlled local authority (4.1(h)).

D) THE ROLE AND POWER OF THE 'OPPOSITION' GROUPS

Groups of councillors in parties in the minority on a council may meet privately to devise their tactics for opposing the ruling group and for developing their own policy plans which they can propose at council meetings.

They will usually have 'leaders' who will be the chief spokesmen and women in leading debates at the main council meetings. The opposition groups may be given some facilities in the council headquarters, for example, a room with a desk and telephone and access to secretarial facilities (see 4.1(e) regarding the appointment of political assistants).

As has been said under 4.1(a), opposition and minority parties will automatically get places on the committees in proportion to their membership on the council. The groups will be able to decide for themselves who those representatives should be and who will speak on different subject areas.

The opposition leaders will have quite a lot of contact with the chief executive and chief officers to enable them to keep apace with policy developments and obtain background information.

Under the Access to Information and Local Government and Housing Acts 1985 and 1989, the opposition groups cannot be excluded from any committee meetings where policies are being decided as they will be guaranteed some representation. They also have open access to inspect documents relating to the council except where 'confidential or exempt' information is involved or in matters where a councillor has a professional or pecuniary interest in the document.

It is important to know who the leaders of your opposition parties are, as at some stage they might win control of the council after elections or hold some balance of power even if they are in the minority. Some decisions will have 'all party' involvement and support, so it is worth ensuring that you have made 'all party' approaches over issues and grant applications particularly in areas where party political control tends to change.

E) ASSISTANTS FOR POLITICAL GROUPS

Under the Local Government and Housing Act 1989, political groups on the council can appoint political assistants if the group has at least 10 per cent of the council membership. There can be no more than three groups on a council with political assistants. (There was no restriction on these appointments prior to the Act.) Also the assistants cannot be paid more than £13,500 a year for one-year contracts only.

F) THE 'GROUP WHIPS' AND GROUP VOTING

Most groups have a machinery for trying to make sure that all the councillors in their group vote for the agreed group policy at full council meetings and on committees. If it is large enough, the group will have a whip, a councillor (elected by the group) who is responsible for maximising the vote in support of the group policy at council meetings and also for aspects of liaison between the group and the council officials. Members of a group are expected to support and vote for group policies although individual councillors may be given dispensation to vote against the group decision on a particular local issue affecting the ward they represent, or on a matter of conscience. In the latter case, this would generally mean members of the group would have what is known as a 'free vote'. Again the group itself will decide whether or not an issue should be given a 'free vote'.

All parties and groups will have different rulings and procedures for using the 'whip' to ensure maximum unity on making decisions.

If a councillor votes against the group he or she could be disciplined and could run the risk of being expelled from the group. This would make it difficult for them to win support for any projects they are involved in, and difficult for them to exert influence on policies being discussed in the group. These problems usually arise within the majority group in control, where every vote may be necessary to ensure that policies agreed by the party in power become the policies of the council.

G) ALL-PARTY ISSUES

As has been said, it is important to stress that many uncontentious or minor issues will not be the subject of a group decision and discussion in private by the group. There will be matters on which there is wide agreement amongst all the parties and where no 'party line' emerges. There are also matters of importance regarding a major planning development or service policy where all parties may agree and support the majority party in its decisions. However, if a party is in control, its views will be dominant and will ultimately direct the decisions a council may wish to take.

H) 'HUNG COUNCILS' – HOW THEY OPERATE

In recent years there has been a shift away from the dominance in local government of the two main political parties, with the increasing involvement of other parties. This has resulted in many local authorities having 'hung councils', where no one party has gained control by obtaining the majority of seats in the election.

There have been many different responses to this by the political party groups involved in a 'hung council'. For a full examination of the way hung councils are dealing with their situations see *The Management of Hung Authorities* published by the Local Government Training Board (Appendix 1).

Obviously the customs of councils managed by a majority group, as described earlier in this chapter, do not always apply. A great deal depends on whether any of the political groups are prepared to support each other to gain an oveall majority particularly on major issues such as the budget and who chairs the committees. In some hung councils the chairs of committees are rotated beween the parties, from one meeting to another, although a party might refuse to take up the chair if they feel they cannot get the support they need to carry through a policy. In some hung councils the chairs are taken by the party with the greatest number of seats but no overall majority. Since the Local Government and Housing Act 1989, the number of seats each party can take on committees is decided according to their representation on the council. This may mean that there is no guarantee that the chair will be supported as the party with the most number of seats could be outvoted by the other parties represented.

'Joint administrations' can be formed between two political parties, giving them an overall majority of seats on a council, but these may not be long-lasting arrangements because unity between two party groups can be very fragile. However, if such an arrangement does appear to exist and is publicly recognised, then you will know for the time being that those two political groups probably have the most control of council decisions. In these circumstances, the other political party groups may go into 'opposition' (see 4.1(d)), refusing to take part in 'all party' discussions or refusing to take their turn in chairing meetings, as decribed above, if they are still formally involved in a rota.

As has been said, the 'chairs' of committees may have far less power in hung authorities than they do in majority party administrations, as described in 3.11, for several reasons. The chair may be rotating, therefore lessening the power and status of the person involved who in a majority council may be in that position for many years building up knowledge, contacts with chief officers and understanding of how the system works. The influence of the chair, even if it is not rotating, may be reduced by virtue of the fact that he or she cannot rely on getting decisions through their committees because they may not have the majority of seats. Therefore, if you have a hung council in your area it is important to recognise the limitations on the role of any chair of a committee unless you are sure that there is a relatively stable 'joint administration' operating.

Many hung councils are operating with party spokesmen or women who may take their turn in the chairs and will be the ongoing spokesmen or women on a particular area of council work. It would, therefore, be useful to find out from your chief executive in a hung council who the party leaders and party spokesmen and women are, and to contact them individually in your lobbying. They may all be involved in the sort of briefings and pre-committee discussions described in 4.2 below leading up to the preparation of committee agenda.

It is vital that you relate to all political parties equally in 'hung councils' because of the uncertainty of who will be in control next. The political groups will operate very much in the way described in 4.1(b) with leaders, whips, etc. It is important to remember that a decision supported by one or two political groups still might fall at the full council meeting if they cannot exert a controlling influence on the final vote. If a committee has agreed to support your organisation's application for a grant, you would still be wise to lobby every member of the council before their full council meeting to try and ensure all party support at that meeting.

Some hung councils have developed 'working practices' and 'conventions' to help the chief officers and councillors in maintaining some kind of balanced approach in dealing with the lead up to decision-making, and in ensuring that some policies are implemented. They may also devise a 'standing order' specifically to deal with decisions which cannot be agreed at a committee by the parties involved. This could result in a large number of decisions actually being made at full council meetings. This is in contrast to councils where majority parties operate where the major policies are usually decided in the main committees and final approval can be guaranteed by the party in control at the full council.

In a 'hung council' situation it is especially important to develop a good working relationship with the chief officers of the council to ensure that they understand the purpose and background of your application for funding or for a policy change. You must clarify with them what is happening to your application at each stage, and if possible attend the meetings where it is being discussed so that you can be clear who you need to meet and lobby for the next stage, remembering that the decision may be reversed at any stage by one or more of the political parties involved.

As there are now a number of hung councils throughout the country, there are some more set responses being developed to these situations, particularly by chief officers, which are discussed in the report produced by the Local Government Training Board (see 4.1(h) and Appendix 1).

I) COUNCILS WHERE PARTY GROUPS DON'T OPERATE

In rural areas, many councils are not controlled by one party with a majority of councillors. In some cases, the main parties are represented but none has a clear majority, in others the council is dominated by 'independent' councillors. In both these situations, the 'group' apparatus is much less influential and decisions may be less predictable, as with 'hung' councils. There may, for instance, be a tendency for more decisions to be made at committee level to be reversed at the full council meetings and for the actual discussions which take place in committee to be more influential in determining its initial decision. The absence of a controlling party apparatus does not mean, however, that all councillors have equal influence. Even on largely independent councils, come councillors or groups of councillors will have more influence than others, based on many factors such as experience, assertiveness, etc. The difficulty is often identifying who these are.

It is also important to recognise that many local authorities in rural areas are becoming more 'politicised', with party groups forming and more people being elected under a party label. In these situations, you may find the council is becoming more like a 'hung council' as described above in the way it operates.

4.2 How committee decisions are evolved

A) THE INFLUENCE AND KNOWLEDGE OF THE CHAIRS OF COMMITTEE

The councillors who chair the committees, and their deputies, tend to have the most power on the committees as they are usually involved in discussions with chief officers before committees meet to discuss the recommendations and the committee reports as well as in planning long-term policy changes and developments. The committee structure is quite hierarchical in this respect, with the 'backbench' councillors tending to be less knowledgeable about the background to recommendations coming to committees. Every local authority will vary according to the style of the chairs and their political group as to how much they involve the councillors in discussions of policy, both in general and on day-to-day matters (see 4.2(e)).

In practice, the chairs of the committees will spend a great deal more time involved in committee work than other councillors as they will be frequently consulted by their officers, not only about policy developments but also about day-to-day problems and crises. Although the chairmanship of committees may be voted on annually in many authorities, the chairs may remain in that position for many years, so building up a great deal of knowledge and experience as well as power. Some local authorities will include automatically all the chairs of their main committees on their policy committee so that they also have a major influence on financial, personnel and general policy matters of the council.

B) PRE-COMMITTEE DISCUSSIONS – WITH OFFICERS

Before most committee decisions are made there is a preliminary process of decision-making which can take several weeks. A proposal or report may come forward from within the council or outside (eg an application for grant aid). It will be considered by various levels of management on the councils, with them giving their observations and opinions at each stage, before it reaches the councillors. For example, if the party in control of the council has included in its manifesto a policy to 'decentralise' a council department, then this proposal will be considered by the chief officers of the department concerned before involving councillors, and possibly others such as trade unions, in developing a policy strategy which could be presented to a committee for their consideration and approval or rejection. The councillors (usually chair and sometimes vice-chairs) may be involved in discussions at an early stage or initiate the idea in the first place (for example, in relation to implementation of a policy backed by the party in control).

When a report to the appropriate committee has been drafted, councillors – again usually the chairs and vice-chairs – will often meet with officers to discuss the implications before it goes to the committee so that they are fully 'briefed' before discussion takes place at committee.

It is important to be aware that there are these many stages of discussion before a proposal reaches an agenda paper at a committee, so it is important to try and influence the proposal at an early stage.

C) PRE-COMMITTEE GROUPS – PARTY GROUP MEETINGS TO DISCUSS POLICY

As well as having discussions about major policies in party groups, each committee meeting may be preceded by a party group meeting to go through the agenda of a committee with the chair, and the group may decide which way they expect their members to vote before the committee meeting takes place. They may also meet to discuss draft reports and recommendations before they are finalised and put to committees. Again, party groups will vary in the extent to which they use such 'pre-committee' discussions to influence the outcome of a decision. It is therefore important to reach councillors before they hold their 'group' meetings where decisions may be made, and then kept to in the open committee.

D) UNDERSTANDING WHEN TO INTERVENE IN THE COMMITTEE CYCLES TO INFLUENCE POLICY

As we have seen, there are several stages in the decision-making process even before a committee meeting takes place to discuss a matter of policy. A policy may be evolving for several months, and stem from party policy, or professional initiatives from chief officers, before the public are aware that is going to be considered by a council committee. It is now possible to be more aware of the background to policy developments with the Access to Information Act enabling you to see background papers with a committee agenda. However, you may find that a policy has already been agreed 'informally' through the processes described before it comes for formal discussion at the committee meeting. This is the first meeting you can attend as a member of the public, unless there has been some form of public consultation about the policy in its developmental stage (see 4.2(e)). This is certainly not the case with all decisions. Some may have come on to the committee agenda with very little pre-discussion by councillors or officers and *many* relatively minor matters may well be undecided before the formal committee meeting takes place, so there are opportunities to get decisions reversed or referred back for more discussion.

Firstly, a decision made by a sub-committee has to be agreed by the full committee and the full council before it is acted upon. At each of these stages a wider group of councillors will be involved in considering a decision and they can seek to refer a matter back for further consideration or amend a resolution. A 'reference back' or 'amendment' must be moved and seconded by councillors before it is considered and voted upon.

So if a decision you are concerned about was approved by a sub-committee, then it could still be defeated, amended or referred back by the full committee or full council. This means you must be aware of the need to lobby councillors at each stage until your objective is achieved.

Secondly, if a proposal has been rejected by a sub-committee, you can lobby the councillors on the full committee and try to persuade them to approve the proposal at the next stage and reject the sub-committee's decision. However, you must find out if your proposal is subject to 'delegated powers' (3.7) because decisions made in this way cannot be challenged or reversed.

E) PUBLIC CONSULTATION – 'STATUTORY DUTIES'

The ability of the public to influence decisions will depend on whether the local authority has developed public consultation practices beyond the formal statutory duties it has to obtain public opinion on various council policies. For example, a highways authority has the statutory (legal) duty to consult the public, police, traders, emergency services and others about traffic orders affecting a street, eg parking, closing off a street, double yellow lines, etc. If an education authority wants to close down a school, it has to issue a public notice informing the public of its intentions, giving them a time limit in which to make objections to the proposals to the education authority which would then be considered by the Secetary of State for Education or the Secretary of State for Wales. If planning permission is being requested for a person to extend or 'change the use' of his or her property, the local planning authority will have to inform those affected by those proposed changes and give them time to object. Often, local authorities will use local newspapers to advertise changes of these kinds as well as sticking notices informing people of proposed changes to buildings affected and holding public meetings. Council tenants have the right to be consulted about housing management policies affecting them under the Housing Act 1980 (consolidated into the Housing Act 1985). This includes such policies as a major scheme for improving an estate, changes in policy concerning repairs and maintenance, services provided in connection with your homes such as alarm and concierge systems for the elderly. However, it does not include policies on rent setting or consultation on how the council's housing budget should be spent. In practice, local authorities can get away with doing very little of this statutory consultation because it is difficult for tenants to know what they have a right to and how the consultation can proceed. This is dealt with more fully in 4.2(f).

If there is a proposal or decision affecting your street, organisation, estate, neighbourhood or school, contact your local councillor, or the chief executive of your local council, to find out about consultation procedures. There may be a further opportunity to object in a public inquiry or if a decision is 'appealed against' by those affected. A local citizens advice bureau or advice centre should also be able to advise you of your rights.

F) PUBLIC CONSULTATION – 'INFORMAL'

There has been a change in the attitude of some local authorities towards public consultation over the past 10 years, with a growing awareness of the frustration people feel about the lack of involvement in decisions and policies which affect their lives. Some local councils have sought to involve people at neighbourhood level in discussing plans for their areas – environmental, housing, recreational, etc, through setting up neighbourhood forums, holding public meetings and putting on public exhibitions explaining proposals. For many years, community action groups, tenants' and residents' groups have been trying to change their local councils' and councillors' attitudes towards this kind of participation.

As has already been said in the previous section about statutory rights to public consultation, we do have some rights to consultation in law, but often they are not followed up very effectively by councils. As far as council tenants are concerned, the variations in consultation are enormous. As a result of pressure from tenants, some councils have forged links with their tenants, meeting them on a regular basis to discuss the policies of the local housing authority. This might involve a committee of councillors and tenants meeting in a local area to discuss how they should spend their capital budget on repairs and improvements. Some councils consult their tenants on rent levels which goes beyond the statutory duties to consult. Others may fund their tenants groups to enable them to function effectively so that they can represent the views of other tenants when meeting the council. The take-up of this kind of consultation is patchy throughout Britain. The establishment of Tenant Participation Advisory Services (see 2.3(c)) alongside national and local tenants' federations has meant that there has been more commitment forthcoming from councils in this area of service. Also, the Housing Act 1988 (see 2.3(c) has pushed some councils into recognising that they must have some kind of partnership with their tenants if they want to keep them and their housing stock. It has started making some councils regard their tenants more as consumers with a less paternalistic, bureaucratic style of management, often developing local neighbourhood or estate housing officers, moving the staff out of the town halls and civic centres.

Another example of the way local authorities have opened up their consultation processes has been through the work of equal opportunity committees concerned with race and women's equality. One of the main features of these local authority committees has been to co-opt people (as has been described in chapter 3) on to the committees to provide a wider representation of views in discussing council policies. The other feature has been the way they have sought to consult women and ethnic minorities through public meetings, forums and surveys about the services their local authorities provide, and to involve them in drawing up plans or making proposals about the way in which local services could be improved to their benefit. This is discussed further in the next chapter.

In chapter 10 we will look at ways you can endeavour to persuade your local councillors and council to involve you in developing policy, planning changes which affect your organisations and committees, and at the ways in which you can challenge the policies they have adopted.

5
Local Government – How to Influence it

This chapter will give practical guidance on how to find out who your councillors are, how to contact them, who it is best to contact in the 'power structures' described in chapter 4, all in relation to councillors' local and committee responsibilities. It will suggest ways in which you can lobby your councillors most effectively and give you some insight into their responsibilities. It will also suggest ways to approach and contact the officers of the council to your best advantage.

5.1 Know who your councillors are

Under the Access to Information Act, your local authority has a duty to provide a public register of the names and addresses of all your local councillors and what committees they are on.

Don't forget that you may have more than one local authority operating in your area, so you may need to contact more than one council, eg district and county, to obtain comprehensive lists for your area.

There is a *Municipal Year Book* which should be available in all public libraries giving the names and addresses of all councillors in England and Wales and all the chairs of committees.

5.2 Contacting your councillors

(i)   When you ring or visit the council to find out who your councillors are, it is often best to ask for the chief executive's department. Most councils will have an officer dealing with 'members services' and they will know the names and addresses of councillors and which wards they are serving.

(ii) You can also address letters directly to the councillors, 'care of' the council headquarters. Your letters will be forwarded to their home addresses.

(iii) Don't be afraid of contacting councillors at their homes. You can ask them if they have 'surgeries' where they deal with complaints and problems. If they do not have surgeries you can ask if you can make an appointment to see them at their house or yours. Councillors should follow up problems and complaints raised by their local constituents.

(iv) It is best to approach councillors who represent the ward you are living in, as they are your publicly elected representatives. So if a group is lobbying the council over a particular issue, it is preferable if members of the group approach each of their own local councillors over the matter.

(v)   You can also tackle councillors on the particular *committee* concerned with the issue you are dealing with. For example, if you are making an application for a grant to the social services department, you can obtain a list of all the members of the committee and contact them individually, making references to your application. The councils should again give you lists of the members on the committees you are concerned with.

(vi) Remember that it is important to speak to the *chairs* and *vice-chairs* of committees as they often have the most influence on a committee in its decision-making, (3.11) or to the party spokesmen and women in 'hung' councils (see chapter 4.1(h)).

(vii) As has been said, you can write to councillors on a particular committee or council and you can deliver letters, addressed to the councillors individually, to the council headquarters, and ask them to be sent out to councillors. You can also do this with annual reports or other publications. It is also possible to ask for reports or information to be placed in the 'members' room' or at the councillors' places in the council chamber at their full council meetings.

5.3 How to get councillors to listen to you

(i) Councillors are busy individuals with many commitments and may appear to be reluctant to get involved in many specific 'causes'.

(ii) It is often difficult to get councillors to attend meetings of outside organisations unless they have been personally asked to speak or address the organisation, or there is a special purpose to the meeting concerning the council. Councillors are often prepared to attend Annual General Meetings of organisations and quite a lot of constructive 'lobbying' can be done at a social occasion when the refreshments are being served!

(iii) A great many councillors cannot attend meetings during the day if they are working unless they can claim an 'attendance allowance' or a 'financial loss allowance' to compensate for loss of earnings. They will be able to claim these allowances for attending their own council committee meetings. It is, however, possible for you to suggest that you might attend one of their council meetings and address the councillors about your work. If you have an audio-visual aid, like a film or videotape, you could suggest that you show the film to the councillors either at the beginning or the end of the meeting.

Note: Some councillors have virtually become 'full-time' in order to concentrate on council work. This is often the case with leaders of councils, mayors and chairs of committees. Councils may give special allowances to councillors in these positions in addition to their attendance allowances. The Widdicombe Report has considered the possibility of having salaried councillors like MPs.

5.4 Lobbying your councillors

(i) Obviously, it is important to be aware of all the different stages in decision-making and the political influences and groupings you will be dealing with, as described in chapter 4, when you are lobbying councillors for a grant or change in policy. It cannot be too clearly stated that it will often be too late to leave your lobbying until the date of the committee meeting when the matter is being finally decided upon. It is important to be lobbying at all stages of pre-committee and group decisions.

(ii) It is important to work from the bottom up and the top down as far as lobbying is concerned. It is often useful to go straight to the top and approach the *leader* of the council and the *chairs* of the major committees involved and ask them to meet you and hear your case. In the case of 'hung' councils, it would be important to contact all the party leaders and their spokesmen and women. It is also important to lobby your local councillors and those on the committee concerned as they can put pressure on their ~leadership and call for support from fellow councillors when a decision is being made at the 'group' meetings.

(iii) Some political 'groups' on councils are prepared to have speakers from outside organisations to put their case on an issue. You could make a request to address the groups in this way by writing to the secretaries of the groups 'care of' the council headquarters. Some councils have now adopted 'open government' policies and are prepared to allow groups to address committee and council meetings during the business of the committee.

(iv) It is important to lobby the councillors in all the parties represented on the council to try and get united support. It is not very helpful for a voluntary organisation to become a 'political football' between the parties, or to be identified with just one political party. This applies to all councils regardless of the nature of political control operating (see point (v) below).

(v) Once you have secured your objective of obtaining a grant or securing a policy change, keep your councillors informed of how your organisation or neighbourhood is benefiting from their decisions. Invite them to your projects, send them reports and thank them for their support. You will *need* it in the future!

A) MEMBERS' ALLOWANCES

These are paid to councillors if they attend council meetings, which are called 'approved duties'. They are taxable and national insurance is deducted. Only one attendance allowance can be obtained over a twenty-four-hour period.

B) FINANCIAL LOSS ALLOWANCES

This is an alternative to the attendance allowance. A financial loss allowance can be claimed if the councillor can prove that she or he has lost earnings. It cannot be claimed for any paid leave given by an employer. It is not subject to tax or NI deductions and there are varying rates according to the number of hours the councillor is involved in an 'approved duty'.

5.5 Dealing with officers of the local authority

(i)   As well as influencing the politicians on a council it is important that you win the support, interest and co-operation of the officers of the department you are dealing with if you are seeking to influence a policy of the council or you are seeking approval of a grant application.

(ii) For many policy issues as well as grant applications, the officers will make a recommendation to the councillors on the merit of the case in professional or technical terms. For example, if you are involved in a group which is pressing for a pedestrian crossing to be provided on a busy main road, the officers will generally make a recommendation based on government guidelines concerning the number of vehicles using the street and the numbers of pedestrians crossing the street at particular times. Councillors can amend the officer's recommendation or make alternative proposals but they do tend to follow many 'officer recommendations'. Officers may also offer advice about a proposal and leave it up the councillors to make recommendations, particularly on matters of general policy involving political decisions.

Some local authorities have adopted 'open government' policies which give you the right to comment on draft reports referring to your organisation or group, before they go to the committee for consideration. It is worth asking whether your council does have this kind of policy and suggesting that it might be helpful for you to see the draft, even if they haven't got a policy on this. You can then check if the draft report is accurate and fair.

(iii) If your case has convinced the officers of its merit and justification, this does not necessarily mean that the councillors will automatically support it. In other words, you really have to ensure that both officers and councillors are convinced. Never stop lobbying councillors and officers until the decision has been made – never rely on spoken assurances from any source, and never feel 'safe' that no more can be done until the 'minute' of the decision is published and you have seen it in writing. Once you have been successful in obtaining a grant, it is important to keep up the liaison with the officers, sending them regular progress reports, your audited accounts and annual reports.

5.6 Dealing with different departments of the local authority

(i) You may find that one department or committee of the council will not help you, if you are making an application for a grant, through lack of finance, or because they do not support your case, or they may disagree with your interpretation of a policy or law which affects you.

(ii) If you are applying for money, you can try approaching another department of the same council, possibly altering the stance of your application in order to reflect the responsibilities of a different department or committee. For example, an application to the education committee for a grant to support a community education theatre group could also be made to an arts committee, if the council has one, highlighting the impact of the project on community arts.

Remember that you will have to start the process of negotiation, consultation and lobbying again with the officers and councillors of the different departments and committees if you are making an application to a different department for a grant.

(iii) If one committee has turned down an application for a grant but you have had some sympathy and support from councillors on that committee, you could suggest that they formally refer the application to another appropriate committee. This will save some time and will show that there is some support from the council for your application, but you will still have to approach the officers and councillors or the committee it has been referred to, in order to gain their support.

(iv) Another reason for turning to a different council department might arise if you find, for example, that you are
getting nowhere in tackling your local housing department
about their policies on homelessness. In this circumstance,
you could approach the legal department of the authority
via the chief executive and/or the council solicitor to
explain why you think the housing department is not
implementing the laws on homelessness.

5.7 Influencing council policy through co-opted members, working parties and open forums

As has already been described, many local authorities have now
made moves to 'open up' local government by co-opting people
on to committees, by developing informal consultation procedures, setting up working parties and holding forums and
public meetings on specific issues.

In whatever area or issue you are concerned with – housing,
education, race, environment or your own local neighbourhood
– there may be a way in which you can influence your council
directly by attending a meeting, forum or obtaining a co-option.
You can press for these opportunities to be made available and,
if they already exist, ask your local authority for details of meetings and for the membership of committees so that you can
influence the way resources are distributed, services are provided and priorities are made.

It must be borne in mind that the Local Government and
Housing Act 1989 now restricts the opportunities for this kind of
influence by removing the rights of co-optees to vote on decision-
making council committees (see 3.2(c)). However, their voting
rights still remain on advisory committees and estate management committees.

5.8 Influencing councils through joint consultative committees

As well as learning to influence your local authorities from 'outside', and trying to influence them through the various co-opted
members who serve on committees (see 3.2(c)), you can find out

who the voluntary organisation representatives are on the joint consultative committees (JCCs).

The JCCs consist of representatives from the health authority and local authorities in your area, and since 1985 voluntary organisations have been entitled to have three representatives on each JCC.

The regional health authorities in England and the Welsh Office organise the election of the three voluntary sector representatives in many cases in the same way as the community health council voluntary sector members are elected. In some areas, a local voluntary organisations forum or council for voluntary service could be asked to organise the elections. It is important to find out who your voluntary sector representatives are, how they were elected, and try and ensure that your organisation is involved in that process in the future.

The JCCs have an important role to play in planning community care and supporting joint finance projects (see 8.2), so it is worth understanding how they work and who is representing your interests. For more information about JCCs contact the *NCVO Community Care Project* who produce a regular newsletter and have published several documents concerned with the role of JCCs and access to joint finance (see appendix).

At the time of writing, the White Paper on Community Care, 'Caring for People', has just been published. There is no indication in the White Paper about how the planning machinery will be developed to replace JCCs, which will cease to exist in the form described in this section after 1991. It is likely to be left up to local authorities and local agencies to develop such consultative planning machinery. NCVO is calling for guarantees about the nature of input from the voluntary sector. The independent sector will be involved with local and health authorities in drawing up community care plans but not in the way that has been developed through the JCCs. Joint finance will no longer be available in the same way as it operates at present (see chapter 8). Although these changes will be implemeted in April 1991, there is likely to be a cessation in use of joint finance and existing mechanisms leading up to the date of implementation.

The White Paper is likely to have a dramatic effect on the role and work of voluntary organisations in the future. Their role will be important in contributing to community care planning. Community care plans will have to be made available for scrutiny by the public giving important information about services which will be made available for users and carers. Local authorities will have to draw up criteria for assessing those with social care needs and publish those criteria showing how the assessments are made.

5.9 Involving councillors in your organisation

A great many voluntary and community organisations invite local authorities in their areas to nominate councillors to sit on their management committees. This is a matter of choice for the organisation itself to decide whether it would be useful to have a councillor involved in this way. The local authority will nominate a councillor; the organisation cannot choose who it is, except possibly if it is for a local community organisation. Then they can suggest that a local councillor is nominated. The constitution of the organisation may allow councillors to be observers or co-optees but not voting members. Again, it is up to you to decide how you want to involve councillors, if at all. It is quite often the case that councillors are not regular attenders of meetings because they are on so many committees and often have clashing commitments every night of the week. However, they will receive agendas and minutes of meetings and could always be asked to attend a particular meeting if something was coming up which affected the organisation or neighbourhood.

Councillors can be useful advocates if they are sympathetic to your aims and objectives. If they are not sympathetic or they want to try and change the way you run your organisation then problems can arise. Sometimes organisations approach a councillor personally who they think would be interested and ask them if they could seek the nomination. If that councillor is in a minority party on the council they may not get the nomination. You will have to weigh up the advantages and disadvantages of inviting a local authority to make a nomination and ensure that you are ready and able to deal with someone who may not be as sympathetic as you hoped. If this is the case it would be advisable to invite the councillor to spend some time with the organisation at her or his convenience to discuss your work and objectives.

Some local authorities will ask to put a councillor or councillors on your management committee if they are funding your organisation to a large extent. It may even become a condition of funding. You may try and negotiate around this by offering some alternative ways of establishing good liaison, for example, by holding a quarterly meeting to which you invite councillors and officers of the local authority to meet with your members and report on your work. Some local authorities would prefer to do this because it would involve less of a regular commitment by one or more councillors but could provide a 'monitoring' function on the way a group spends its money. Partnership and contractual arrangements developed with local authorities through funding will be looked at in the next section and in chapter 8.

5.10 Local authority involvement in voluntary organisations registered as companies or industrial and provident societies

The Local Government and Housing Act 1989 has introduced controls on those voluntary organisations which are registered as companies or industrial and provident societies and in which the local authority is involved. These controls are important to consider if a voluntary organisation is setting up and thinking about legal status. They should be taken into account if you have councillors, officers or others associated with a local authority (see 5.9) involved on your boards and management committees or in your membership. The government's reasoning behind the introduction of these controls was supposedly to prevent local authorities setting up voluntary organisations which they could influence or control, to circumvent government legislation, eg privatisation. However, the consequences for independent voluntary organisations which have no intentions of this kind, and have been working closely with and funded by local councils for years, are considerable if they are registered as companies or industrial and provident societies.

The government defines three kinds of companies which could be subject to controls:

A) LOCAL AUTHORITY CONTROLLED COMPANIES
These could be companies which are direct subsidiaries of local authorities, or the council controls the majority of seats on the board and votes at general meetings. Some companies falling in this category could be identified as 'arms length companies' if

they meet certain conditions laid down to restrict the council's involvement. These involve such restrictions as limiting the number of local authority directors to no more than one-fifth and restricting financial dependence on the council.

If a voluntary organisation *did* fall within the controlled company definition, it and the local authority would be severely restricted in their relationship. For example, the organisation could not carry out any functions which the local authority itself could not undertake. The same capital and revenue restrictions which apply to the council would be extended to the voluntary organisation, eg the spending limits under section 137 (see chapter 8).

B) LOCAL AUTHORITY INFLUENCED COMPANIES

Companies where both a fifth or more of the voting members of the company or board are associated with the local authority, *and* half or more of its business is connected with the local authority, are deemed to be 'local authority influenced companies'.

Local authority association extends beyond just councillors and officers to include employees of local authority controlled companies and anyone who has been a councillor in the last four years. So involvement of any of these people on the board of a voluntary organisation which is a company which does half or more of its business with the local authority might mean that the organisation is deemed to be 'local authority influenced'. Furthermore, the Secretary of State has the power to extend the definition of local authority association to spouses of councillors, office holders in political parties and consultants, if she/he thinks local authorities are using these types of association as a way of exerting influence on a company.

The Secretary of State will have considerable power to make regulations governing how these companies will be regulated and controlled in their relationships with local councils. Once the regulations have been defined, the council will have to check up that the companies are abiding by them, otherwise any financial arrangements they have with them will be illegal.

It is likely that some of the restrictions laid down for controlled companies will apply to 'influenced companies', eg the organisations affected will have their capital borrowing counted against the council's capital limits and they would therefore have to get permission from the council to borrow capital for buildings or equipment.

Councils will have to be constantly checking up to see if organisations fall into these categories as memberships and directorships change. This could be very intrusive and could have a negative effect on the relationship between the local authority and voluntary organisation.

At the time of writing, the government has agreed to consider exemptions for voluntary organisations which can show themselves to be independent from the council and can 'demonstrate their independence'. They will not be subject to controls if they can convince the government of this independence and gain an exemption. They would have to prove their independence by showing 'a combination of the terms of the company's constitution, charitable status and membership of a national grouping of voluntary bodies which demands that its members be independent'.

NCVO in its Briefing Note (2 November 1989) identified the following situation where companies would be exempt according to the government's consultation paper:

(1) Local authority controlled companies – exemptions
   (a) Groundwork trusts
   (b) Other bodies largely financed by Central Government eg Regional Tourist Boards, Area Museum Councils, Regional and Area Arts Associations
   (c) The National Housing and Town Planning Council *and* others on application to the Secretary of State.
(2) Local authority influenced companies – exemptions
   (a) Independent voluntary organisations where
      (i)   the company is established solely for charitable purposes;
      (ii) fewer than half the directors are 'associated' with the local authority;
      (iii) the local authority concerned declares that the company is managed independently of the local authority; and
      (iv) the local authority concerned declares that they have not taken into account in settling the terms of any transaction with the company any borrowing or capital expenditure proposed to be undertaken by the company.

(b) A company which is a member of a national network, where
   (i) the criteria for membership demonstrate independence from the local authority;
   (ii) the network is undertaking 'quasi-statutory' functions (to be defined).
   To date, the National Association of Citizens Advice Bureaux is the only network which the Government has agreed under this category. Furthermore the draft circular only refers to networks of advice agencies under this category; however, the Government accepts that a number of others will also qualify. NCVO intends to argue that the exemption should also apply to other networks and is therefore drawing up a proposed list of networks for exemption in consultation with others.
(c) All voluntary organisation companies in receipt of £2,000 or less in any one year from the local authority.
(d) Registered housing associations.
(e) Building preservation trusts registered with the Architectural Heritage Foundation.
   and individual companies on application to the Secretary of State.

For further clarification on this contact NCVO and WCVA (see appendix).

C) MINORITY LOCAL AUTHORITY INTERESTS

In addition to the above two categories, there will also be companies where the council has a minority interest. Local authorities will not be allowed to have a minority interest in any company without the approval of the Secretary of State. However, current indications are that an exception will be made for virtually all types of voluntary organisations.

The controls introduced in the Local Government and Housing Act 1989 have many implications for voluntary organisations if implemented unsympathetically. They could jeopardise funding arrangements and constructive partnerships which have developed between a voluntary organisation and its local authority.

6
Making an Application for a Grant

This chapter provides a practical example of how to use the council most effectively. It gives an explanation of the stages through which the application will have to go to obtain approval or rejection.

6.1 Stages in the grant-making process

STAGE 1
Establish which department and committee is likely to consider your application. You can do this by ringing the chief executive's or town clerk's department and explaining what your application is for, and they should tell you which department to submit the application to and which officer to contact.

STAGE 2
Once you have established which officer/department you should be dealing with, contact them directly and ask when the application has to be submitted and in what form (for example, by completing an application form or writing a report in sub-

mission). It is important to make sure that you have been given 'closing dates' for submission. This is particularly important with some government grants such as Urban Aid (see 8.1(a)), because councils have committee meetings which do not necessarily tie into the time given by the Department of Environment and Welsh Office to receive applications. As is explained in chapter 7, estimates are drawn up early in the financial year to be approved by councillors in the autumn, so it is advisable to start your discussions with a local authority early in the financial year, which starts each April.

STAGE 3

Offer to meet the officers to discuss your application so that they can be fully informed of your needs. They can often give you some ideas as to what would be most acceptable to the councillors, in terms of budget, etc or style of application (see 5.5). You can ask if you can see their report in 'draft form' before it goes to the committee to check it is accurate and puts your case fairly.

STAGE 4

When you have drawn up your application, send it to the chief executive/town clerk and to the director of the department concerned, with covering letters to these officers. Make sure the layout of the report is clear and readable and, if possible, include a copy of your latest annual report or a report on your activities. Also include audited accounts, if you have any.

STAGE 5

You can also send the application to the chair and vice-chair of the committee concerned; the leader of the council and any councillors you think may be sympathetic. You may wish to send the application to all the members of the committee concerned, but it may be preferable to send a letter to them summarising the application, with some information about your project.

Near the date of the committee meeting, contact the key councillors on the committee and ask them what their views are on the application and if they would like any further information. You can also ask them if they will be supporting you, and can try to ascertain how much support there is, if any, for the application. Also, check with the officers how the other departments are receiving your application, eg, legal, finance, equal opportunities, to see if any problems have arisen.

STAGE 6

It is useful to attend the committee meeting, as members of the public, to show your concern for getting the application through. You can approach the councillors as they go into the committee room and tell them which organisation you represent. Your presence will make them more mindful of your applicaiton. Sometimes local authorities will allow groups to come and present their applications to the councillors. It is worth asking if you can. The local press might be there and you may wish to make a statement to them, depending on which way the decision has gone. It is always better to give them a written statement so that you can check you have been quoted correctly.

STAGE 7

If your application has been rejected, there is always the possibility of getting the matter reconsidered or referred back for further consideration. You would usually have to produce some additional or new points which could be made in support of your application, but, as an alternative, you could attempt to convince them that there would be consequences if they didn't make the grant to you. If the application has been rejected at a sub-committee stage, it could be reconsidered at the full committee, or it could be 'referred back' or 'taken back' by the chair at the full council meeting. If it is 'referred back' by a councillor for further consideration, a vote will be taken as to whether she or he will be supported in the 'reference back'. The chair can personnally 'take it back' for further consideration at the council meeting when she or he is 'moving' the minutes of the committee meetings. If the application has been rejected altogether at the full council meeting, under the standing orders of the council it may not be eligible to be reconsidered for a specified period of time, unless a councillor specifically requests a reconsideration (see 3.9).

STAGE 8

If your application has been accepted by a sub-committee, it could still be voted against at a full committee meeting or at the full council meeting, through the mechanism described above. It is possible that a councillor could move a vote against the decision to give you a grant at either of these points. This is why you have to nurture an application right through all the stages, mindful of how the 'group in control' are thinking, and trying to find out if opposition is likely at any stage. You can never feel confident until the grant has been agreed by the full council and has therefore completed all the stages of decision-making.

STAGE 9

Some local authorities, for example, the London Boroughs Grants Scheme, have an Appeals Procedure for organisations whose grant applications have been turned down. Ask your authority if they have such a procedure operating when you first submit the application.

Note. It is preferable to have a decision 'referred back' for further consideration than voted against altogether, because it gives you more time for 'lobbying'. So it is more useful to get sympathetic councillors to refer a matter back for further consideration than for them just to vote against the recommendation not to give you a grant, unless they can be sure of winning that vote.

6.2 Summary of stages

1. Consult officers about dates of meetings, time limits, etc, and the style of your application.

2. Inform councillors of your application.

3. Ask the officers if you can see their draft report of your application before it goes to the committee. Check the progress of the application as it is discussed by different departments on its route to the committee.

4. Attend the committee meeting where the application is being discussed.

5. Check with supportive councillors and officers whether there is any likelihood of the application being referred back or voted against.

6. Turn up at full committee and full council to check that it is being approved.

7. If your application is not approved by a committee, try and get a supportive councillor to refer it back at the next stage for

further consideration, or for a changed decision in favour of your application. Lobby all the councillors to try and get the decision reversed or reconsidered.

8. Obtain a copy of the minutes stating the decision of the council as far your grant application is concerned.

9. Appeal against the decision if there is an Appeals Procedure available.

For further information see *Negotiating Grants* published by NCVO Community Care Project (see appendix).

7
Local Government Finance - How It Works

Local government finance is currently undergoing a profound change which is affecting almost every aspect of the way that local authorities fund their activities. Domestic rates have been replaced by a poll tax (community charge), business rates are now set by central government rather than by local councils, there are new controls on various aspects of spending by councils and so on. The starting date for most of these changes is April 1990, as far as England and Wales are concerned, although it will be several years before all the changes are fully implemented and their implications are clearly in evidence.

This chapter seeks to provide an overall view of the new system and identify some of its main features, together with a brief comment on the special case of housing finance. The changes need to be seen against the background of government policy in the 1980s towards local government finance of increasing regulation and control. The government believes that the new finance system, in particular the poll tax, will make local authorities more accountable to their electorates, but others believe that its true significance lies in the further centralisation of decision-making and decline in the power of councils (see introduction).

7.1 Types of spending

Local authority spending is divided into two categories:
- **Capital spending** – this is spending on physical assets which have a long-term value, eg purchase of land, construction of buildings and roads, major items of equipment.
- **Revenue spending** – this is spending on the day-to-day provision of services, eg salaries and wages of staff, running costs of buildings and facilities.

Capital spending generally relates to large one-off items whilst revenue spending is primarily concerned with items which are recurrent from year to year. Local authority estimates and budgets make a clear distinction between these two and they are subject to different controls and financing arrangements.

7.2 Capital spending

Capital spending has always been subject to some degree of government control, although the form of control has changed several times. The new system is enshrined in the Local Government and Housing Act 1989 and is based on controlling local authority borrowing. Borrowing has always been important to local authorities as a means for financing capital projects and a control on borrowing provides a significant constraint on spending.

Under the new system, a local authority is allowed to finance capital spending in four principle ways:

A) BY BORROWING UP TO ITS CREDIT APPROVAL LIMIT

Each year, all local councils are given a basic credit approval by the government, a figure which sets a limit on the amount they may borrow to finance general capital projects. In addition, they may be given supplementary credit approvals for specific projects or schemes which the government supports. It is important to note that a credit approval enables the council to borrow from one of the standard sources, such as the public Works Loans Board. It is not a cash grant; the council has to pay interest and repay the loan by its expiry date.

B) BY USING CAPITAL RECEIPTS

Capital receipts are the sums which an authority receives when it sells off an asset, such as land or housing. Under the new system, an authority has to set aside 50 per cent of any sum it receives towards paying off its oustanding debts (75 per cent in the case of receipts from council house sales). It can use the rest to finance additional capital expenditure beyond the credit approval level.

C) THROUGH CAPITAL GRANTS
The government and the EEC make grants towards the debt charges on specific capital projects which fall within the remit of certain progammes, for instance the Urban Programme. If a council receives such grants, its credit limit would get increased accordingly. However, such grants often only cover part of the total cost of a project which the authority has to top up from some other source.

D) USING PART OF THEIR REVENUE INCOME
Councils now have more or less full discretion over the extent to which they make use of this option, although this will depend on other pressures on their revenue budgets. (See Revenue Spending below).

It should be noted that certain kinds of short-term property leases do not count against an authority's credit approval limit although the provisions here are complex. It is possible that leasing provides a further option for acquiring property in particular circumstances.

Local authorities can make grants from their capital budget towards capital projects being undertaken by voluntary and other bodies either in the form of a simple direct grant, or as part of, for instance, an Urban Aid capital project. Such grants probably require more planning and programming than revenue grants, and any request will be in direct competition with other capital projects which the authority wishes to undertake that year. Nevertheless, they can be an important source of funding for voluntary organisations and other bodies.

7.3 Revenue spending
Revenue spending is by far the larger of the two categories of spending. An authority's revenue budget covers expenditure on the day-to-day provision of services, education, environmental health, old people's homes, parks, etc. Although the budgets will

differ from council to council, the main elements will include:

- **Staffing** – salaries and wages will be the largest element of the revenue budget, exceeding perhaps 50 per cent of the total.
- **Premises** – the cost of maintaining and running the council buildings.
- **Vehicles** – all authorities maintain fleets of vans, minibuses, etc.
- **Materials and supplies** – books for schools, cleaning materials, food, office equipment etc.
- **Capital financing** – the repayments of principal and the interest on loans borrowed for capital expenditure together with any direct contributions to the capital budget.
- **Grants** – to outside organisations and voluntary bodies.

A council's estimate of revenue spending is based on figures calculated for each of the main departments, which are then added together to provide an overall total. One major exception concerns housing, for which councils have to maintain a separate income and expenditure account known as the Housing Revenue Account. This shows its own surplus or deficit. See *Housing Finance: A Basic Guide* published by Shelter (appendix). Expenditure on an authority's direct labour organisation is treated in a similar way.

7.4 Financing revenue expenditure

Under the provisions of the Local Government Finance Act 1988, a local authority has four sources of finance to run its services: the poll tax, government grants, business rates and the charges it makes for its services.

A) THE POLL TAX

The poll tax is a flat-rate tax which is payable by most adults over the age of 18. The tax is collected by the local district council (or London borough) on behalf of itself and of any higher tier body such as a county council. Each council decides the level of its poll tax on an annual basis, taking into account the amount of money it will receive from other sources and issues such as its policies and popularity with the electorate. Although councils are free to set the poll tax at any level, the government has the reserve power to limit the amount if the tax falls within the criteria of what the government deems to be 'excessive'.

There are three kinds of poll tax:

- **Personal** – This is the one which applies to most adults, subject to certain exemptions and rebates (see below).
- **Collective** – This is paid by landlords/owners/managers of certain short-stay accommodation such as bed-and-breakfast hotels and some residential hostels run by voluntary organisations such as long-stay hostels. The landlords/owners/managers collect contributions from residents calculated on a daily basis.
- **Standard** – This is paid by the owners of second homes and of property which is vacant for three months.

(i) Exemptions

Although few in number, some categories of adults have been exempted from paying the poll tax. These include: prisoners, the 'severely mentally impaired', 18-year-olds still at school, patients in hospitals or nursing/residential care homes on a residential basis, residents of short-stay hostels for the homeless, persons of no fixed abode, volunteer care workers such as community service volunteers, monks, nuns, diplomats, etc. Students have to pay 20 per cent of the poll tax levied at their term-time address.

When the poll tax provisions were going through Parliament there were calls for exemptions from many groups particularly concerned with residential care such as women living in Women's Aid refuges. There was also much concern about the position of elderly people living in the community with relatives/'carers' who would have to pay the personal community charge but who would be exempted if they were in residential care (see above). After much pressure the government agreed to exempt people living in short-stay accommodation and also exempted the organisations providing the accommodation from any form of community charge. However, the definitions of who falls within that exemption are still not clear. Women's Aid refuges were exempted from collective community charge, so there are many anomalies in the way exemptions have been granted at the time of writing.

(ii) Rebates

Some adults who are liable for the poll tax are able to claim rebates of up to 80 per cent from the local council. In general, this provision relates to those in receipt of income support or have an equivalent low income, although it should be noted that individuals are assessed on the basis of family income, not personal income. The government is raising income support levels to take the remaining 20 per cent into account. However, this increase is calculated on the basis of the national average of poll tax which will not help those in areas of higher than average poll tax bills.

(iii) Community charge register
Chapter 12 gives information about how the community charge register is compiled and what your rights are to see the information it contains. Each district council has to compile a register of all those liable to pay. It must also appoint a community charge officer who has powers to impose fines on anybody refusing to supply the personal information required and to take to court those who fail to pay the charge, the court having a number of ways of ensuring payment at its disposal. Individuals have a right of appeal against a decision of the CCRO to include them on the register, etc, and such appeals are heard by a Valuation and Community Charge Tribunal (see chapter 12). NCVO and NCCL have both produced guides to the poll tax (see appendix).

B) GOVERNMENT GRANTS
Government grants are generally an important source of revenue finance for local authorities and the principle grant is the revenue support grant. Each council receives an annual revenue support grant decided on the basis of how much the government thinks an authority in a particular area should spend on its services. In order to do this, the government has to carry out a 'standard speaking assessment' for each area based on a few key factors, and the grant which it then announces is, in its view, sufficient to enable a council to meet these needs without levying an 'excessive' poll tax. The revenue support grant replaces the old rate support grant. It does not take into account any assumptions about the wealth of the area in terms of its tax base and is a simple, fixed sum.

In addition, there are a number of other much smaller specific grants made by the government to local authorities such as transport grants, education support grants, the Urban Programme, etc. These are for specific projects for which the councils generally make particular submissions.

C) UNIFORM BUSINESS RATE

Although householders no longer pay rates, the rating system still exists for businesses and organisations. The main difference now is that the level of the rate is set nationally for England, and separately for Wales, by the government. Councils have no say in deciding what the rate should be and receive a share of the total sum raised strictly in accordance with their population. The government's intention is that uniform business rate should only increase from year to year in line with inflation. From the point of view of local councils, the business rate has become similar to a government grant.

The government carried out a revaluation of the business rate prior to introducing it which has resulted in rateable values increasing on average by 800 per cent. (See chapter 8 for information about rebates for voluntary and charitable organisations.)

D) CHARGES

Local authorities make charges for some of their services and facilities, for example car parks, home helps, swimming baths, adult education, school meals and hire of halls. These form a significant part of a council's income and are an important policy issue each year. Councils have discretion to charge what they wish in most cases. Income from council house rents goes into the housing revenue account and is treated separately.

The Local Government and Housing Act 1989 does give local authorities the power to introduce charges for any services apart from education, police, the fire service, elections and for some library services (see 2.3(d)).

7.5 Housing finance

Housing finance has been subject to special regulation from some years and the extent of this has further developed under the recent changes. The most important changes include the 'ring-fencing' of the housing revenue account. Revenues from rents go into a special housing revenue account (HRA), not the general accounts of the council, and the HRA has to balance income and expenditure. Under the new system, councils will not be able to subsidise the HRA from its other sources of income, so that housing activities will have to become more self-sufficient.

7.6 Information about council finances

Details of a local authority's spending plans and its accounts are available to the public through two main documents:

A) ESTIMATES

The council's estimates of expenditure are produced in advance of the financial year to which they relate, the process of formulating the budget generally beginning in the previous September/October. The financial year starts on 1st April. The estimates break down the revenue budget, giving expenditure by departments and sub-sections of the council, with main headings for each department, eg staffing. Details of capital expenditure are also given in the estimates.

B) ANNUAL REPORT AND ACCOUNTS

Each council has to publish an annual report of its main activities during the financial year just finished, and this report has to include its completed accounts for that year. These can give a valuable picture of the council's financial situation. Sometimes the annual report is included as part of a civic newspaper which may be distributed to all households in the council's area. Local authorities also have to send out a leaflet explaining their budget and spending plans with the rate demand to all the ratepayers in the area.

8
Sources of Finance for Voluntary Organisations from Local Authorities

This chapter will summarise in outline the sources of funding which are available from local authorities. It will also deal with the implications of the Local Government and Housing Act 1989 in relation to funding for voluntary organisations. In each piece of recent legislation lies a minefield of obstacles and restrictions for voluntary organisations making it difficult to understand the grant-making process.

8.1 Grants involving central and local government funding

A) URBAN PROGRAMME
The major source of joint funding of voluntary organisations by central and local government is the Urban Programme. Urban Aid was established under the Local Government (Social Needs) Act 1969 and the Inner Urban Areas Act 1978. Urban

Aid provides joint funding from the Department of the Environment in England and the Welsh Office (WO) in Wales, and from a local authority, for a limited period of time. The local authority pays 25 per cent and the government pays 75 per cent of the grant. Grants can be given for capital and revenue projects.

Urban Aid can fund projects of various kinds – social, economic, environmental. In England, Urban Aid is available for organisations based in local authorities which have various designations, according to levels of deprivation. The money is available only in the Inner City Partnership and Programme Authorities which are known as the Inner Area Programme (IAP). In Wales any district or county council can apply for Urban Aid. The NCVO practical guide *Government Grants: A Guide for Voluntary Organisations* gives details of which authorities have IAP Status (see appendix).

Urban Aid grants can be applied for every year. In Wales a circular from the government is published and sent to all local authorities. Voluntary organisations can obtain a circular with application forms from their local authorities or the WO. The form has to be completed by the voluntary organisation, sent to the council for their consideration, and, if the council accepts the application, it will be sent to the WO. There is usually a restricted time period to get through all these stages, so groups have to be sure they get their applications ready to be considered in time.

In England new arrangements were made in 1986, with an IAP cycle which starts in March and takes the local authorities and voluntary organisations through various stages in drawing up and submitting applications over a year's period. The local authorities have to draw up a 'strategy' aimed at dealing with social, economic and environmental needs in their areas, including priority areas. They will have to decide, in discussion with voluntary organisations, which projects they want to sponsor as part of the IAP. These will be submitted to the DoE who will decide how much money (capital and revenue) they will allocated to the local authorities. The local authorities will then decide how they distribute this allocation.

The emphasis of the Urban Programme has been increasingly to focus on economic development, the environment and capital projects for both local authorities and the voluntary sector. Priority is not given to 'social service' type projects and in the latest Circular in Wales, the percentage of grant aid which will be allocated to voluntary organisations is defined. Projects which can show themselves to be fostering 'self-help' initiatives for the unemployed are still looked on favourably.

B) SECTION 11 OF THE LOCAL GOVERNMENT ACT 1966

Some areas of England and Wales qualify for grant aid under Section 11 of the Local Government Act 1966, which gives funding to local authorities for projects which concern Commonwealth immigrants in their areas. Funding is provided on the basis of 25 per cent local authority contributions and 75 per cent Home Office contribution and the funding is not limited to a certain time period, but it is available for staffing costs only.

The Home Office has issued a Circular (No 72/1986) which enables local authorities to obtain this funding to employ workers who can then be seconded to voluntary organisations providing a certain service in the community. These are called 'detached duty' posts. For example, workers could be seconded by a local authority to a Women's Aid group running a refuge for Asian women.

The 1986 Circular requires local authorities to draw up 'strategies' for meeting needs and fulfilling their duties under section 71 of the Race Relations Act 1976. The local authorities are asked to consult those organisations which represent people who will benefit from the strategy to discuss their proposals for section 11 posts. In drawing up plans for 'detached duty' posts you will need to consult the relevant ethnic minority organisations about your proposals, such as Councils for Racial Equality. Section 11 money can be granted at any time of the year by the Home Office, but it may be advisable to submit applications when a local authority is considering its budgets (ie during the autumn) unless it is prepared to consider applications from voluntary organisations at any time during the year and has a budget system which enables it to make decisions on grant aid throughout the year.

NCVO and the National Association of Community Relations Councils have produced *Section 11: Funding for Black and Ethnic Minorities? Guidance Notes for Voluntary Groups*. These set out clear guidelines on the use of section 11 by voluntary organisations for these posts. It is important to note that these are local authority posts – the workers are not employed by the voluntary organisation. The workers are seconded to the voluntary oranisation so great care must be taken in drawing up a Code of Practice and/or guidelines as to how the arrangements will work as the worker's formal line manager will be in the local authority. The application itself has to be submitted by the local authority although of course this must be drawn up with the full involvement of the voluntary organisation or community group.

Several local authorities have drawn up guidelines about these posts for their local black and ethnic minority groups and examples are given in NVCO's Guidelines. Care must also be taken in looking at the long-term future of these post in terms of how long the section 11 funding will be available and who will take it over when it ceases. At the time of writing section 11 funding is under review and there is a possibility that the government may amend it to enable grants to be given directly to black and ethinic minority groups.

C) URBAN DEVELOPMENT CORPORATIONS

The government has set up Urban Development Corporations (UDCs) throughout Britain as part of their policy for tackling derelict land and buildings where traditional industry has declined, for example in Dockland areas. UDCs have been set up in the London Docklands area, Merseyside, the Black Country, Cardiff, Teeside, Tyne and Wear, and Sheffield. There are mini UDCs in Bristol and Leeds.

These bodies are appointed by the government to redevelop areas using a mixture of public and private money. They have considerable planning powers and can in some cases replace the local authority's planning and housing functions in the affected areas. Some of them have local authority representation on the boards of the corporations. In other areas, local authorities have declined to take up seats on the boards and have opposed the government in declaring UDCs. The UDC in each area has to produce a strategy for development. Local authorities and other interested groups such as voluntary organisations and community groups, as well as businesses and other commercial interests, should be consulted about this.

There has been some recognition that there should be more consultation with local people living in UDC areas because of the unpopularity of some of their policies in the way they affect local communities. NCVO organised a seminar to look at these issues and local development agencies and councils for voluntary service are trying to set up consultative bodies and groups to ensure that the voluntary sector and local community groups are heard. At the time of writing it is difficult to assess the success of these moves.

The UDCs have made money available in grants to voluntary organisations, particularly for 'one-off' capital projects. Each UDC has its own criteria for giving grants and so it is worth contacting your UDC to see whether you can apply. It is likely that you will not get a grant if you are working outside the UDC area and unless you can show that your work benefits the areas of the UDC.

8.2 Joint finance

Voluntary organisations can get money from joint finance, a scheme which involves the local authorities and the health authorities with money from central government. Joint financed projects are recommended by the joint consultative committees (see 5.8) which voluntary organisations sit on, alongside the local statutory authorities. Joint finance has been available since 1977 and the JCCs bring together local authorities, the health authorities and voluntary organisations to help them jointly to plan their services and comment on their effectiveness.

Every year, projects will be considered by the JCCs with statutory authorities' applications considered together with those from voluntary organisations. Funding will be given for a set period of time, with three years at 100 per cent. The local authorities will gradually have to 'take on' responsibility for the full funding of the projects and government support should stop after seven years.

Projects concerned with housing and educational provision are eligible, as well as health and social services projects.

Not many voluntary organisations may be aware of the possibilities of obtaining funding under joint finance. However, now the JCCs have voluntary orgsnisations represented on the committees, you can contact them to find out when applications are being received, and you can take the opportunity of explaining the aims and objectives of your project, and ask for feedback on the JCCs activities.

As has been described in 5.8, the use of joint finance is likely to change under the provisions of the White Paper on Community Care published in November 1989. The move towards the 'contract culture' involving the voluntary sector is examined in 8.8.

The JCCs will be 'serviced' by one of the local authorities represented on the committee or by the health authorities, so you should contact your local authority social services department and ask for the person who deals with 'joint finance', because they will have an officer advising the JCC on the applications it receives. Remember that most statutory authorities start drawing up their budgets each autumn before the new financial year, so you ought to be making enquiries about joint finance in the spring of that year.

8.3 Care in the community

For projects which are directly concerned with transferring health care services to the social services, for example, services designed to help people with learning difficulties out of hospital into the community, grants may be given by the government to local authorities and voluntary groups for up to 13 years, with 100 per cent funding for 10 years. In Wales this sort of funding is available under the 'All Wales Strategy for the Development of Services for Mental Handicapped People' initiated by the Welsh Office. Voluntary organisations can apply for 'care in the community' funds but they have to do so after close discussion with their local health and social services departments. In Wales funding is also available in this way under the 'Elderly Initiative' also sponsored by the Welsh Office. These schemes do not have to be approved by the JCCs. The future of all these initiatives is likely to change with the implementation of the White Paper on Community Care.

8.4 Joint funding and collaboration

In addition to joint finance initiatives, local authorities can work together to fund a voluntary organisation, without government or health authority money being involved. This often happens where the project has relevance to more than one local authority, eg single homeless projects concerning both a district council and a county council (housing and social services). It might require a great deal of negotiation with councillors as well as officers to get this sort of collaboration, unless there are already mechanisms to make it work. The suggestion for joint support might come from the voluntary organisation or community group itself. A great deal will depend on the co-operation which can be fostered between authorities in dealing with funding applications of mutual interest.

8.5 Direct local authority grant aid

Local authorities can give grants to voluntary organisations under various powers given to them under Acts of Parliament. Grants can be obtained from different committees of the council, according to what the purpose of your application is and how it fits in under the various responsibilities of the different council departments. This section will look at a) some examples of what some council committees are able and likely to fund. It will then go on to deal with b) wider powers which a council has to fund grants to voluntary groups which do not easily fit in under any of the committee budget heads. It will deal with c) the new Economic Development power introduced in the Local Government and Housing Act 1989 which gives councils the powers to fund voluntary organisations concerned with economic development, and also mention a new advice power included in the 1989 Act.

Section 8.7 will deal with the latest restrictions on local authority funding of voluntary groups under the Local Government Acts of 1986 and 1988 (political publicity and promotion of homosexuality).

A) APPLICATIONS TO SPECIFIC DEPARTMENTS/ COMMITTEES

If your project or grant application does appear to be linked very clearly to one of the spending departments of the council, you will probably find that the committee has a grants budget for voluntary organisations and uses its powers to assist projects of your kind.

(i) Social services (county councils, metropolitan districts, London boroughs)
Under section 65 of the Health Services and Public Health Act 1968, social services departments have the power to make grants for voluntary organisations. Social services departments also will have budgets for organisations such as playgroups, which

would have been granted to them by a sub-committee specifically concerned with child care.

(ii) Housing (district councils, metropolitan districts, London boroughs)
Under section 73 of the Housing Act 1985 (formerly Housing (Homeless Persons) Act 1977), it is possible for local district/borough councils to give grants to voluntary organisations who are in some way helping the homeless. This can be 'revenue' funding (see chapter 7) or they can help with provision of premises (eg a refuge for Women's Aid), furnishings, and staff time and support.

Voluntary organisations involved in 'special needs' in conjunction with housing associations can get grant aid (hostel deficit grant) from the Housing Corporation (Tai Cymru in Wales), often in conjunction with local authority financial support. This is under review at the time of writing. Further information can be obtained from the Special Needs Housing Advisory Service (see appendix for addresses).

(iii) Education (county councils, London boroughs, metropolitan districts)
The education authority will have a budget for giving grants to voluntary organisations concerning educational projects, eg holiday playschemes, youth projects, camps, play centres under the terms of the Education Act 1944.

(iv) Parks/leisure/sport/arts (county councils, district councils, metropolitan districts, London boroughs)
Under section 19 of the Local Government (Miscellaneous Provisions) Act 1976, local authorities can give grants via their parks and leisure departments for voluntary oranisations concerned with play facilities. Some local authorities may have 'sports committees' which give grants specifically to sports groups/organisations and activities. Also some councils will have arts or cultural services committees which give grants for arts projects and activities.

(v) General grant-giving committees
Apart from the specific grants you can apply for from different 'service' committees, most councils will have a general grant-giving committee which can give grants to a wide range of organisations for projects, events and activities which do not fit

any of the particular committees we have mentioned (see 8.5(b) for powers used).

When you are thinking of applying for a grant it is worth ringing up the chief executive's department and asking if they have a general grants committee. This may be a function of the policy committee or one of its sub-committees. You can also enquire whether they have a separate sports or arts committee where it may be more appropriate to direct your application. There may also be women's or race equality committees with budgets for grant giving to voluntary organisations. The chief executive's departments should advise you as to the most appropriate committee and may have an application form for you to complete. Make sure you find out when your committee will be considering your application.

B) POWERS TO GIVE GRANTS TO VOLUNTARY ORGANISATIONS

Some specific Acts of Parliament have been mentioned above which give local authorities powers to fund voluntary organisations for various activities and services. 8.5(c) deals with section 137 of the Local Government Act 1972 which has been used extensively for funding projects with more general purposes.

It is becoming increasingly important that local authorities and voluntary organisations work together to find out which powers are most suitably used for funding their projects to avoid some of the restrictions brought in by the government on use of section 137 and the restrictions introduced in other pieces of legislation such as the restrictions in the Local Government Act 1988 on publicity and campaigning (see 8.5).

NCVO have produced a guide on the powers available, *Getting in on the Act* (see appendix). Some examples of powers that can be used are as follows:

(i) Section 111 of the Local Government Act 1972
This power enables a council to fund anything which is concerned with the functions, powers and responsibilities of the local authority itself. So anything to do with housing in the voluntary sector can be funded using this power in conjunction with Housing Act powers. Equally anything to do with education and social services could be funded in this way.

(ii) Section 71 of the Race Relations Act 1976
This power can be linked to a specific power and to section 111 and can then assist in funding black and ethnic minority projects concerned with local authority functions.

(iii) Section 141 of the Local Government Act 1972 and section 88 of the Local Government Act 1985
A research power which could be used to fund voluntary organisations (not available for district councils).

(iv) Section 142 of the Local Government Act 1972
An information power which enables councils to fund much of the work of advice and information-giving agencies. The government has now amended this power to include a more specific advice giving power in the Local Government and Housing Act 1989. This means that local authorities will be able to use this power to fund a wide range of advice-giving agencies such as citizens advice bureaux, advice centres and law centres.

There are other examples relating to specific services and to particular types of activity and services which a voluntary organisation is providing. Again, reference to the NCVO publication mentioned above will give you guidelines on what you can suggest.

C) ECONOMIC DEVELOPMENT POWERS UNDER THE LOCAL GOVERNMENT AND HOUSING ACT 1989

Under the new Act, a power has been created for councils to promote actively economic development in their areas. Details of the levels and conditions attached to this are included in the regulations made under this Act.

The government allows councils to give grants to 'public undertakings' which are involved in promoting economic development. They have said that this can include voluntary organisations that are involved in co-operatives, training schemes and small business initiatives although voluntary organisations are not specifically mentioned in the Act. The implications of this are that some voluntary organisations which have been receiving support under section 137 (see above) may now get funding under this new economic development power.

In addition to the new funding powers, the government has

laid down that councils must draw up an economic development plan for their areas each year showing how they intend to use this new power in their spending plans and what they hope to achieve as a result of that investment. In drawing up the plan they must consult organisations concerned with economic development. This could include not only businesses, but also voluntary organisations and projects. This may give the voluntary sector more of a chance to shape the way the funding is directed. It should certainly give them a voice in the planning and may give their funding more security.

D) FUNDING IN LONDON AND THE METROPOLITAN DISTRICTS

The Local Government Act 1985 enabled the successor authorities (see 2.2) to come together and establish a joint grant scheme for voluntary organisations if they are serving more than one borough or metropolitan district. These are called section 48 schemes, eg the London Boroughs Grants Scheme. If you live in a London borough you can contact the LBGS to see if you would be considered eligible for a grant. There is a link with the London Voluntary Services Council which has a forum which monitors the scheme. The LBGS does have an appeal system. If you live outside London in a metropolitan district, Tyne and Wear, West Yorkshire, Greater Manchester and West Midlands all have these schemes.

The Local Government and Housing Act 1989 in its early stages in Parliament tried to introduce new controls on the section 48 schemes which would have made them difficult to operate, but they were eventually reprieved. However, the government has reduced the section 137 limit (see 8.5(c)) per adult head for London authorities to the level which they think section 48 schemes could have fallen under the section 137 powers. (Contact NCVO and the London Voluntary Services Council for up-to-date information.)

E) WIDER POWERS TO FUND VOLUNTARY GROUPS UNDER SECTION 137 OF THE LOCAL GOVERNMENT ACT 1972

As has been said, voluntary organisations have been able to apply for grants which do not fit in clearly to any particular committee/department of the council. This has often been done under Section 137 of the local Government Act 1972. Many councils have general grant-giving committees, often under the finance or policy and resources committee of the council. Until April 1990 section 137 allowed councils to fund projects of this kind, which were considered to be of benefit to the inhabitants of the area, up to a limit of the product of a 2p rate. This has been changed under the Local Government and Housing Act 1989 following replacement of the rating system with the Poll Tax.

The new limits on section 137 spending are £3.50 per adult head in parish councils, £2.50 per head in shire districts and county councils, £5.00 per adult head in the metropolitan districts and councils with one tier only such as London boroughs but only £4.00 per head in metropolitan areas where there is a section 48 scheme operating (see 8.5(e)). These limits are not linked to inflation and can only be changed by an Order made by the Secretary of State.

Under the 1989 Act there is an exemption from the limits described above for schemes that get some of their funding from another government source, eg the Urban Programme or from the EEC.

However, some councils and therefore voluntary organisations are going to lose out with these changes, especially London boroughs and shire districts where there is a high rateable value. There may be ways of finding other powers to fund some of these schemes (see 8.5(a)) or through the new Economic Development Power (see 8.5(c)). It is unclear at the time of writing how many projects will lose out, but it will hit hardest those areas where section 137 has been used a lot and where there has been a high income from the old business rate (now replaced with the uniform business rate (see chapter 7).

8.6 Rate relief

Prior to the Local Government Finance Act 1988, charities and voluntary organisations which rented or owned their premises could apply to the local authority for rate relief.

With the introduction of poll tax (see chapter 7), non-residential premises owned or rented by charities, and those organisations established for charitable purposes only, and voluntary organisations – eg offices, shops, community centres – will come under the new nationally determined 'uniform business rate'. Under the new system charities will receive 80 per cent mandatory relief from their rates. Local authorities will still have the power to grant up to 100 per cent relief to voluntary organisations regardless of whether they are charities.

VOLUNTARY ORGANISATIONS PROVIDING RESIDENTIAL SERVICES

If you are running a residential service, eg a hostel or Women's Aid refuge, you will not be rated in this way. Some residential organisations of this kind will be subject to the collective community charge (see chapter 7), eg long-stay hostels. Others will be exempt from the collective community charge but the residents will have to pay their own personal community charge (Women's Aid refuges) and others will be exempt from any form of community charge altogether (eg short-stay hostels for the homeless). See chapter 7 and the NCVO guide to the Local Government Finance Act 1988, *Responding to Rate Reform* (see appendix).

8.7 Government restrictions concerning publicity, campaigning and the promotion of homosexuality

This section deals with the restrictions which were brought in under the Local Government Act 1986 regarding political publicity and the effect this has had on funding voluntary groups, particularly those concerned with campaigning. It deals with amendments to the 1986 Act contained in the Local Government Act 1988 and looks at the implications of the clause which was introduced regarding the promotion of homosexuality (now section 28).

The Local Government Act 1986 may restrict a council's right to fund activity which is publicising a campaign. The Act was brought in specifically to stop local authorities promoting publicity campaigns which could be identified with a particular political party. It also attempted to prevent a local authority from publicising matters which are not the direct responsibility or 'proper concern' of local government. As a result, the Act also specified that councils should not fund or support voluntary organisations which undertake these kinds of activity.

NCVO has produced detailed guidelines for voluntary groups on the new restrictions, including section 28 on homosexuality, in *Publish and Still Not Be Damned* (see appendix).

The Local Government Act 1986 included a test to see whether a publicity campaign or activity could be described as 'party political'. The test was very vague and subjective, and involved considering whether a 'reasonable' person would look at some publicity and think that it was designed to show support for a particular political party. In the 1988 Act, the test remains but six factors have been identified in section 27 (which include the above test and other points in the 1986 Act) which are supposed to be used to determine whether the publicity material has passed the test. These are concerned with such things as the content and style, the timing and circumstances of the publicity, whether there is any reference to a particular politician or party, whether it supports a point of view which is clearly identified with one political party and the effect it was likely to have on people who see it as part of a campaign.

The 1988 Act also requires councils to take note of codes of practice introduced by the government concerning political publicity. The Department of Environment has produced a *Code of Recommended Practice on Local Authority Publicity* (Circular 20/88) which has been reproduced in the NCVO booklet referred to above.

As regards the clause on the promotion of homosexuality (known originally as clause 28, now section 28), this prohibits a council from intentionally promoting homosexuality. Clarification of what this means may only come in a test case but it has been suggested by legal opinion that it means councils must not encourage people who are not homosexual to become homosexual (see *Publish and Still Not Be Damned*). Again, legal opinion suggests that this should not interfere with the promotion of equal opportunities through projects which try to deal with discrimination against lesbians and gay men. It should not usually affect arts festivals, social activities or information about gay and lesbian groups given in directories. NCVO suggests that in applying for funding for projects of this kind, it is worth emphasising the objectives of tackling discrimination and providing a service. A lot will depend on how willing the council is to work with you to make the grant application fall within the law and support your organisation financially. If there are already well established procedures for voluntary organisations to make grant applications with the assistance of council officers, and there are local councillors who are prepared to back you, then your projects and activities may still get funding despite the restrictions of section 28.

It is clear that the legislation can be very widely interpreted on the issues of political publicity and section 28, so it may be unnecessary to limit activities. However, some councils may use it as an excuse not to fund certain voluntary organisations. Some voluntary organisations aware of the new restrictions may not think it is worth applying for a grant from their local council any more. This is not the case and the limits must be pushed with the assistance of organisations like NCVO which may be able to advise you (or your local CVS or other local development agency).

NCVO gives some useful tips about how to approach these restrictions in the booklet referred to above, showing how you can word your application in such a way as to avoid the traps of the Acts. For example if you are running a welfare rights campaign or information campaign on a new law, you can put the emphasis on 'information', spelling out the implications without attacking particular politicians or parties. You can promote equal opportunities and pursue positive action programmes. If you find you are getting no help from unsympathetic council officers, you will need to identify support from local politicians. The problem with the legislation is that it can make people afraid of taking a stand and worse, it can bring out and confirm prejudices. There is no doubt that many grant applications have not seen the light of day because of these factors.

It is important to remember that voluntary groups can also fund this sort of activity through other sources, apart from the local authority, so if you can identify another source of funding which will fit these particular projects there should then be no danger of breaking the law. However, there may be particular conditions attached to other sources of funding which you must watch out for.

Another important issue regarding these restrictions concerns the powers under which the council can fund you. The 1986 Act introduced a measure to restrict local authorities from funding voluntary organisations promoting publicity and information campaigns which were not related to the functions of the local authority (restricting section 142 of the Local Government Act 1972). Also, this restriction has been tightened further by case law to include 'persuasive' material. In addition, the 1986 Act has restricted the use of section 137 of the Local Government Act 1972 (see chapter 7) so that it could not be used to fund voluntary groups on projects just concerned with publicity. It is important, therefore, as has already been said in this chapter, to look closely at the powers your project could be funded under. A helpful council should be prepared to do this and with your help increase the chances of you getting a grant.

8.8 Funding through 'contracts' with the local authority

There have been changes in the past few years in the relationship between many voluntary organisations and local authorities with the increasing emergence of a 'contract culture' as a result of government policy and legislation. Many local authorities and voluntary organisations have chosen to define more clearly their roles and relationships with respect to funding, particularly if the voluntary organisation is supplementing mainstream council activity or providing services which the council has a duty to provide but is not meeting. Also, some councils are developing partnerships with voluntary organisations to provide a particular service together, sharing management and resources, eg in funding and managing family centres for social services departments.

As discussed above, voluntary organisations have always filled the gaps where councils have not fully met their duties under various Acts of Parliament – particularly in relation to housing and social services. For example, the duty to provide temporary accommodation to the homeless brought in under the Housing (Homeless Persons) Act 1977 has been met in the main by voluntary organisations such as Women's Aid, Cyrenians, etc. Other activities concerned with parks and leisure (eg adventure playgrounds), waste disposal and recycling, respite and day care for the elderly, day care and nurseries for the under fives, holiday playschemes) have been provided sometimes exclusively by voluntary organisations and community projects.

Councils have often taken these services for granted and voluntary organisations have had to battle for resources and recognition. In some local authorities there is slowly developing a recognition of the role these organisations play and a closer partnership is developing. This has often resulted in closer links in relation to management, but it can also result in more secure funding arrangements.

There has been a growing emphasis on 'monitoring and evaluation' in the voluntary sector, with some local authorities working more closely with the projects they support to enable some evaluation to take place as part of the funding package. This may contribute to a sharpening up of the organisations' goals and service.

Understanding of these changing relationships leads us to look at the role of voluntary organisations in meeting needs and providing services which the council has a duty to provide. The government has been endeavouring – through the mass of local government legislation it has been pushing through in the past 10 years – to change the role of local authorities from being the main 'providers' to being the 'enablers'. This means co-ordinating the provision of services in an area which can be provided by organisations other than themselves via either privatisation or through developing the role of the voluntary sector.

'COMPETITIVE TENDERING' UNDER THE LOCAL GOVERNMENT ACT 1988

In the next few years some voluntary organisations may be pulled, however unwillingly, into the arena of competitive tendering. This subject cannot be given justice here but is dealt with more fully in the following publications: *Partners or Rivals?* and *Bidding for Change?* (see appendix). However, it is an area of immense importance in considering the funding of voluntary organisations by local authorities as some voluntary groups might find themselves providing part of a service that has to go out to tender under the 1988 Act. As described in chapter 2, only eight areas of council activity at present have to go out to tender under the Act, but there may be more to come. While some local authorities are resisting these changes, there is little they can do but try to ensure that their departments win the contracts.

Other councils are welcoming these changes, not just through the Local Government Act 1988, but also through other recent legislation such as the Housing Act 1988 which enables them to consider the voluntary transfer of their housing stock, to another body so relinquishing their role as a major public sector landlord. This has major implications for those who are concerned with the homeless and special needs housing, also housing advice services who have secured funding from their local district authorities because of their housing functions and duties. In these cases, the housing authority will not necessarily have the resources to fund refuges and hostels run by voluntary organisations.

Under competitive tendering it is possible for voluntary organisations themselves to take a more assertive role in 'bidding' for tenders or parts of tenders, so replacing a funding arrangement with a contract for work to be done. All these issues are being confronted by voluntary organisations now and need examination by those receiving grant aid at present from their local authorities in every sphere of activity. NCVO is looking into this with other voluntary organisations in a working party on contracting out, which produces a quarterly bulletin *Contracting – In or Out?*

9
How to Make Complaints About Local Authorities

This chapter will deal with the steps you can take in raising a complaint about treatment you have received from your council – starting with writing to the chief executive, chief officers of the departments concerned and you local councillor. It will go on to deal with the local government ombudsman and what steps you have to take to raise a complaint with him/her.

9.1 Making a complaint to your local councillor or local authority

If you have a complaint to make concerning the way you have been treated as an individual, or the way in which your organisation has been treated by a local council, it is important to contact your local councillor first and explain the matter to him/her. It is useful to put the complaint in writing and send a copy to the chief executive of the council and to the chief officer of the department concerned, eg the housing manager/director if it involves a housing complaint. You could also send a copy to the chair of the committee involved; in this case it would be the housing committee chair.

If you have difficulty in putting your case in writing, contact your local advice centre or citizens advice bureau for their assistance. You might find it is worth discussing with them first whether they think you have got a complaint which should be dealt with by your local council. For example, you may have a problem which the local council has no powers to deal with because it is government policy, or you may be approaching the wrong local authority.

You may want to write 'in confidence' and ask that your complaint is not considered in public at a committee. Some complaints will be dealt with by the chief officers and leader or chair of the committee concerned, but others might be taken to a committee for consideration. Some councils have a complaints officer who would initially deal with all complaints coming from the public to the council.

If you think you might be able to or might want to take legal action against your local council, consult a solicitor first (see chapter 11).

9.2 Going to the local government ombudsman

If you do not receive a satisfactory answer to your complaint from your local council, in terms of an explanation and/or apology if appropriate, you can contact your local government ombudsman.

The Commission for Local Administration (the body where the ombudsmen are based) describes its main objective to be 'the investigation of complaints of injustice alleging maladministration by local, water, and police authorities with a view to securing both satisfactory redress and better administration'.

There are three local ombudsmen in England and one in Wales, and it is their function to investigate complaints referred to them by members of the public. The complaint does not have to be referred to the ombudsman by a councillor: you can make a complaint directly to the ombudsman. However, the way is also open for you to involve a councillor, if you know of one who is prepared to back your case.

Complaints can be investigated by the local government ombudsman concerning all local councils, joint boards or committees formed by local authorities, police authorities, the land authorities and water authorities. Community or town councils are not open to investigation unless they are acting on behalf of local authorities.

Complaints can be investigated concerning the actions of committees, councillors or officers of the local authorities.

Complaints cannot be investigated about matters of general policy affecting all or most of the inhabitants of a particular area - eg, the level of rates charged and, in general, complaints about commercial transactions or the awarding of contracts for goods, etc, cannot be investigated. However, complaints about transactions involving the purchase or sale of land and compulsory purchase orders are open to investigation.

Complaints cannot be investigated by the local government ombudsman if the matter has already been brought before a tribunal, or come before a court of law or a government minister (see chapter 11). Also it is unlikely that the ombudsman would investigate a complaint where the complainant does have the right of appeal or the right to go to the courts and she or he has not used it, but exceptions can be made.

Complaints must normally be made to a councillor within 12 months of the day when the complainant realised she or he was aggrieved by a decision or action of the local authority. Again, this time limit can be varied if the local government ombudsman thinks it is justifiable to do so.

The sort of complaints which will be investigated relate to 'maladministration' by the local authority. This concerns the way a decision has been made. The leaflet produced by the Commission for Local Administration in Wales explains it as follows:

Maladministration may be taken to cover administrative action (or inaction) based on or influenced by improper considerations or conduct. Arbitrariness, malice or bias, including unfair discrimination, are examples of improper considerations. Neglect, unjustifiable delay. incompetence, failure to take relevant considerations into account, failure to establish or review procedures where there is a duty or obligation on a body to do so or the use of faulty systems are examples of improper conduct. The Local Ombudsman has no power to question the merits of a decision taken without maladministration.

Some examples of maladministration described in the annual report of the Commission for Local Administration are as follows:

Housing
- delay in dealing with an application for a repairs grant
- failure to repair a council house found unfit for human habitation
- failure to inform a complainant that his housing benefit had been withdrawn due to a previous over-payment

Planning
- failure to notify the complainants, contrary to the council's normal practice, of a neighbour's planning application to build an extension
- failure to ensure that a developer of a housing estate complied with the approved plans

Social services
- failure to make regular assessments of the progress of a resident in a hostel for the physically handicapped or to provide suitable rehabilitation, education and training

Environmental health
- failure in removing material containing asbestos from a complainant's home

THE PROCEDURES
A complaint can be made by an individual or group of people to the local government ombudsman. A complaint can be taken up on behalf of a person who has died or cannot act for him or herself. This provision has been publicised recently as a result of representations made by NCVO particularly regarding complaints concerning social services where it may be difficult for a client/consumer to take up a case with the ombudsman without support from a voluntary or self-help group. NCVO has written to major voluntary organisations reminding them that they can make use of this provision, to pursue a complaint on behalf of an individual or a group of people.

Normally the complainant would first contact the chief executive of the local authority or the department involved, and if this action does not remove the grievance, then the person making the complaint should ask a councillor of the local authority to take up the matter with the council, as described in 9.1.

If this still does not clear up the matter, the complainant (or those acting on behalf of him/her) can pass the complaint on to the local government ombudsman directly, or involve a local councillor if they wish. When the complaint is presented to the ombudsman, the following information must be provided:

- Name and address of the complainant.
- Name of local authority concerned.
- Details of the complaint, stating the alleged 'maladminis-tration', (giving dates/names of councillors and officers involved).
- Copies of relevant correspondence and any other docu-ments.
- Account of the way in which the complaint has been brought to the attention of the authority.
- A request that the matter be referred to the local government ombudsman.
- If the matter is outside the 12-month time limit – the reasons why must be given.

THE INVESTIGATION

The ombudsman will decide, firstly, whether or not he or she can investigate the complaint. If it does fall within the criteria for investigation, the ombudsman will inform the complainant, the councillor (if one has been involved), and the local authority that he or she is proceeding with the investigation.

The ombudsman will give the local authority involved the chance to comment on the complaint and on any allegations which may arise.

The ombudsman will send his or her completed report to the complainant, the councillor and the local authority concerned.

If the ombudsman does find that someone has been aggrieved as a result of maladministration, then the ombuds-man's report, having been forwarded to the council, must be considered within three months of it being received. (This can be extended if the ombudsman agrees.)

If the ombudsman is not happy with the response from the council, or not satisfied with action taken, if any, she or he may send a further report to the council with recommendations for action. If again this does not get any response, the ombudsman can require the council to publish a statement giving the recommendations of the ombudsman and an explanation from the council why they haven't acted upon them. This statement has to be published in local newspapers. If the council fails to carry this out, the ombudsman can get the statement published and make the council pay the costs incurred.

These provisions also apply to organisations and committees who are acting on behalf of the council or closely connected with the council, with a few restrictions, (see 5.9).

The Commission for Local Administration in England has revised its booklet in several languages: English, Hindi, Urdu, Bengali, Punjabi and Gujerati. These can be obtained from the addresses given below.

For further information contact:
Commission for Local Administration in England
21 Queen Anne's Gate
London SW1H 9BU
Tel: 01-222 5622

There are three local commissioners (ombudsmen) in England
- Greater London, Essex, Kent, Norfolk, Suffolk, Surrey and Sussex
- the South, the West, West Midlands, Leicestershire, Lincolnshire and Cambridgeshire
- the North and North Midlands

and:
Commission for Local Administration in Wales
Derwen House
Court Road
Bridgend CF31 1BN
Tel: Bridgend (0656) 61325/6

9.3 Making a complaint under the Education Reform Act 1988

Under section 23 of the Education Reform Act 1988, complaints can be made to governing bodies of schools and the local education authority about a wide range of issues concerning your child's education. Complaints cannot be made about the actions of a teacher or headteacher under this section. If a complaint is made in this area, and was brought before the governing body and the LEA, it would be up to them to consider whether disciplinary action was justified.

The complaints referred to in section 23 relate principally to the national curriculum and the provision of religious education and worship in a school. Complaints can be made on all aspects of the implementation of the national curriculum: exemption of courses, withdrawal of pupils (from part of all of the national curriculum), external qualification courses, etc.

LEAs have had to draw up procedures for dealing with these complaints following consultation with governing bodies. Most LEAs will advise you to go to the headteacher first to try and settle a complaint informally, but then you should have recourse to your governing body and the LEA which will designate an officer to deal with complaints under this section of the Act in a more formal way.

If you do make a complaint of this kind and it is not settled informally after discussions with the headteacher, you should put the complaint in writing to the designated officer in the LEA. You can find out who this is by contacting the LEA and asking to speak to the Schools Section. The designated officer should reply to your complaint and inform you whether the complaint will be dealt with by the governing body or the LEA. If the governing body considers your complaint, you should be allowed to attend a meeting to make a presentation about your case, and the governing body should inform you and the LEA of the outcome of their investigation.

If you are not satisfied with the outcome or your complaint concerns the LEA and not the governing body, the LEA will investigate your complaint. A panel will be appointed to consider your complaint including county councillors and again you will be able to go and speak to the panel about your complaint. All parties will be notified of the outcome of the complaint. If you are still not satisfied with the outcome, you can complain to the Secretary of State for Education of Wales.

The procedures for dealing with these complaints may vary slightly from one LEA to another. There will be separate procedures for dealing with complaints about religious education and collective worship for voluntary-aided schools. Also, there may be a statutory appeals procedure which could apply in relation to your complaint. You would have to exhaust this procedure before turning to section 23 of the Education Reform Act 1988 to make a complaint in the way described here. If the Statutory appeals procedure does not allow you to take your appeal to the Secretary of State, you may be able to follow the procedure outlined in raising your complaint with the governing body and LEA.

Contact your LEA, find out who the designated officer is and ask for a copy of their procedure under section 23. The complaints received will be monitored and the education committee should receive a regular report about the complaints. You could also ask for a copy of their latest report.

10
How to Raise Support for a Campaign

This chapter will look at ways in which you can get support in trying to deal with a complaint or a campaign which you, your neighbourhood, or your organisation is involved in, concerning the local council.

It will suggest ways in which you can use public meetings, petitions and the press in publicising your cause.

10.1 Contacting your MP

Although members of Parliament are not elected to represent citizens over local government matters, they often have contacts with the local authorities in their constituencies (both councillors and officers), and they can be useful in getting support for a particular case or problem. If the local MP gives his/her backing to an organisation, group or individual, then it can add weight to an application for funding or to a request for an investigation into a grievance or disagreement about policy. Most MPs have regular surgeries in their constituencies, and the local authority can tell you what their local addresses or contact numbers are.

Your MP will usually have a local agent who will arrange surgeries and deal with some of the local commitments of the MP. Find out who the agent is by contacting the political party to which the MP belongs. You may find you can make an appointment with the MP through their agent at one of the MP's surgeries.

You can contact the agent or the MP directly and ask them if he or she will receive a delegation concerning your campaign or problem. If they agree to this, it is worth contacting the press (see 10.5(d)) and suggesting that they take a photograph of the MP receiving the delegation.

It is worth keeping your MP informed of your activities if you are a local voluntary organisation working in their constituency. You can send them reports of your work, invite them to your Annual General Meetings, and invite them to visit your projects. They may not be able to attend, but at least they will know about your work which may be helpful if at any time you have a funding crisis.

10.2 Contacting your local advice, community or law centre

Throughout England and Wales there is a network of local community and advice centres which are not run by the local authority, but they may receive some or all of their funding from them.

Many of these centres have been set up and are managed by local people in an area. They can become a focus for community action in those communities, advising people of their rights individually but also helping people come together to tackle an issue which may be affecting a whole area, eg traffic conditions, broken pavements, lack of play facilities (see appendix for address of the Federation of Independent Advice Centres).

In addition, the citizens advice bureaux (CAB) provide a comprehensive service throughout England and Wales, offering a wide range of advice to individuals and providing a rota of solicitors who give free legal advice to people with problems and complaints which might include complaints concerning the local authority (see chapter 11).

There is also a network of law centres in England and Wales which provide legal advice and support, with legally qualified workers available to inform and advise you of your legal rights (see the *Law Centres Federation Journal*, published by the Law Centres Federation and *Using Civil Legal Aid*, published by the Legal Action Group (LAG), listed in the appendix.

10.3 Contacting particular pressure and action groups

You may find that there are various pressure or action groups concerned with areas or interests in common with you who could act on your behalf or support your case. For example, a Women's Aid group applying for a grant could seek support for their work from other women's organisations. They could write to the chief executive of the local authority supporting your application, or to their local councillors , expressing their support for you. If you have a grievance with a council over a matter such as a housing problem, you could find out if there are any housing action groups or advice centres in your area who would support you.

You should be able to get a list of local groups of this kind from your local library or from the CAB.

10.4 Other organisations to contact

There may be organisations established in your area which could specifically help you with your problem or project. For example, if you are a group of mums waiting to set up a playgroup, you would want to contact your local Pre-School Playgroups Association (PPA). You would be able to get their address from your local library or CAB, or from your local authority.

There may also be an organisation set up in your area to assist voluntary organisations, eg a council for voluntary service 9CVS), which would give you support, advice and possibly access to photocopying machines and other useful equipment. NCVO and WVCA will supply you with names and addresses of such organisations (see appendix for address).

10.5 Taking action to raise support

A) PETITIONS

Local authorities receive many petitions calling for support for a project or organisation or calling for a change in policy, opposing a decision that has been or is likely to be made. If you draw up a petition, make sure that the people affected sign the petition, and that you do not have signatures from friends and relatives outside the area concerned. It is also important to have individual signatures and addresses, and not just one house-holder signing everyone's names in the household. The state-ment at the top of the petition should preferably be clearly typed. It is advisable to make copies of the petition before you hand them in to the council so that you have a record for future reference.

If you have managed to gather a petition together and you want to present it to the council, it is useful to ask the chief exec-utive if you can present it to the chair of the committee con-cerned with the matter you are raising, at the beginning of the committee meeting where it is being discussed. You can also make this request to your local councillor, especially if they have expressed support for your campaign. They can approach the chair of the committee for you, but it is still wise to put it in writing.

Your local councillor might like to present the petition on your behalf to the chair of the committee. This can be helpful as it often shows that your local councillor is publicly supporting you.

You could ask to present the petition at a full council meeting with all council members present if you have not succeeded in getting your point over at the committee stage, or if you want to bring it to the attention of the full committee for their consider-ation.

Alternatively, you could arrange to hand over the petition at a particular site where the problem occurs, eg on a piece of dere-lict waste land you are wanting to improve, or on a busy main road where you are complaining about traffic conditions, or at a play area where the play equipment has disintegrated. Wher-ever you decide to hand the petition in, contact the press to see if you can get a photo in the local paper.

B) PUBLIC MEETINGS
If you decide to hold a public meeting, you should consider what you hope to achieve from it. If you want to seek support for a cause, an organisation, a group or for a change in policy by the local authority, you must judge whether a public meeting will bring out your supporters or opponents. Quite often, if people support something, they do not bother to attend a public meeting, but if they definitely do not want something to happen, they will turn up and make their feelings known. This can obviously be used against you if councillors or officers or members of the press are there, even if there are hundreds more at home supporting your case. However, a public meeting can be a useful way of testing out opinion before you have decided which course of action to take. It can be useful if you know that there is widespread support for a concern about an issue. It is also important to enable people to put their views and feelings over to councillors and those responsible.

It is vital to organise a public meeting efficiently:

- by making sure that those affected or who may be interested have been have been invited in good time by means of a leaflet or as a result of a door-knocking exercise;

- that you are aware of the difficulties facing women and elderly people in attending public meetings at night, in the dark (if at all possible, you should put an address and/or telephone number on your leaflet or posters asking people who need transport or an escort or a baby-sitter to contact the telephone number). It might also be worth having a meeting in the daytime as well as in the evening;

- that you plan the way the meeting is going to be run in advance, with an agenda for business to be discussed with an experienced Chair. If speakers are to be invited, they should be given good notice of the meeting and be told how long they can speak for and on what subject;

- that you inform the press of the meeting if you want publicity, and, if possible, tell them about the issues prior to the meeting (as mentioned above if the meeting is poorly attended or poorly organised, publicity could not be to your advantage);

- decide whether you want to invite your local councillors to the meeting and, if appropriate, officers of the local authority involved in the decision. Quite often officers will bring charts, maps, slides or exhibitions to explain a policy they are pursuing. If the purpose of the meeting is to raise support for challenging that policy, then it is useful to have your own 'case' well worked out to put to the meeting and the councillors and officers of the local authority.

C) SURVEYS AND QUESTIONNAIRES

As it is often difficult to attract people to a public meeting, it is sometimes useful to go door to door round a neighbourhood with a questionnaire or survey to find out people's views about a particular issue. This may be helpful in deciding whether or not you should hold a public meeting. You can present the findings of the survey/questionnaire to the local council in the form of a report and perhaps invite councillors and officers from the council to meet a small delegation of people to discuss the report.

To do all this requires time and support from local advice and community centres, so it is worth finding out if there is an agency in your area which would be prepared to help you in this way.

D) USING THE MEDIA

You can sometimes secure support through the local newspapers, TV and/or radio stations, but you have to be wary of how you use the press.

- It is often advisable to establish links with one or two local reporters who show interest in your organisation, or the issue you are involved with, rather than relating to a large number of reporters who you do not know.
- If you are submitting an application to a local authority for funds, or asking for a change in policy, it is useful to prepare a press statement outlining your reasons and explaining who you are, and to give the statement to the reporters at the council meeting where the matter is being discussed or to deliver it to the press prior to the meeting.
- If a sympathetic article appears in the paper, it is worth informing the named reporter of developments.
- If you feel your case has been misrepresented, you can contact the reporter who wrote the article and explain where you feel she or he has got it wrong.
- Beware of making 'off the cuff' statements over the telephone or if you are questioned by a reporter at a committee meeting of the local authority which you may be attending. If a reporter telephones you for a statement and you're not sure what you want to say, tell him/her to ring back in 10 minutes or more, to enable you to collect your thoughts and write down a statement or to consult a colleague.

- If you do not want to answer their questions at any point simply say 'No comment' and politely terminate the conversation. Make sure that your organisation has agreed that this is the line of approach you want to take so that no one is caught 'on the hop', because reporters can usually find the names, telephone numbers and addresses of everyone involved in an organisation or campaign. It is often a good idea to have one person who will deal with the press who will quickly learn by his/her mistakes.
- If you do have press coverage, keep a scrapbook of cuttings for future reference.
- If you find difficulty in raising any interest from the press, from your statements or contacts with them, write a letter to the editor of the local newspaper, putting your case and arguments in the form of a letter (usually not more than 200 words). In fact, several people can write to the editor in this way, so as to ensure that at least one gets published. The advantage of this method of getting publicity is that you can control what is said.

For further information and guidance on using the media see *Voluntary Organisations and the Media; An NCVO Practical Guide* (see appendix).

11
Taking Action Through the Courts, Tribunals, Appeals Procedures and Inquiries

11.1 Legal advice and aid in taking action

If you think you have a complaint against a local authority you can go to an advice centre, CAB or law centre, as described in chapter 10, or you could go straight to a solicitor who could give you free legal advice, if you qualify, and, in some circumstances, legal aid to act for you in court. Legal aid is only available to individuals, however, who are personally affected by a decision. It cannot be obtained by a group of people with a general grievance.

Your solicitor will be able to tell you whether you qualify for free legal advice and assistance after assessing your income. If you are on supplementary benefit or receiving Family Income Supplement (Income Support and Family Credit from April

1988) or on a low income, you are likely to be eligible, but your capital (savings) are taken into account in this assessment. You may be eligible for some legal aid advice and assistance, but contributions may also be required from your income. The limits change annually, and your local advice centre would be able to give you some idea as to whether you would qualify before you approach a solicitor. Most solicitors operate under the legal aid scheme. Advice agencies are not supposed to recommend particular solicitors to people. However, CAB and some advice centres do have solicitors giving free legal advice on a rota, and they can take up cases in their own practices as a result of giving advice.

It is important to recognise the extent of legal support and advice which can be obtained if you have a solicitor who is prepared to make full use of the various legal aid schemes available.

The various parts of the scheme you could use are as follows:

A) THE FIXED FEE INTERVIEW

This gives you £5.00 worth of a solicitor's time (up to half an hour), available through the Law Society. You can ask your solicitor for a fixed fee interview if you want to find out whether or not it is worth pursuing a case/complaint further.

B) LEGAL ADVICE AND ASSISTANCE (GREEN FORM SCHEME)

This enables you to have two hours worth of a solicitor's time for non-matrimonial matters, and is calculated according to your income and savings. The Legal Aid Board will give you extensions of this scheme to cover all your legal expenses for a tribunal except for actually representing you at it (except for the Mental Health Tribunal) (see 11.2). So you could get all the advice you need in preparing for a tribunal if the Legal Aid Board sees it as reasonable. The same applies for planning appeals and inquiries. It can pay for legal advice but it cannot cover the costs of legal representation at the appeal or inquiry.

There has been a White Paper about legal aid and advice and a Consultation Paper particularly relating to the Green Form Scheme. At the time of writing, comments were sought on this consultation document, the results of which may lead to a change in the law over the next year. The issues raised in the consultation regarding the Green Form Scheme concern the

proposals to franchise work done at present by solicitors under
this scheme, to a limited number of solicitors, law centres and
possible advice agencies/centres who may specialise in particular types of cases which occur under the Green Form Scheme.
The Legal Aid Board is conducting the consultation and they
raise various options for contracting out work in this way or
developing franchises. They recognise the areas of 'general
practice' and 'specialist' work in relation to these possibilities of
contracting work to particular firms of solicitors and/or
agencies. Issues of geographical accessibility and the need to
protect the funding of voluntary organisations running advice
services are being addressed in the response to these proposals,
and there is widespread concern amongst advice agencies about
the implications of some of these proposals. Contact the Legal
Aid Board and/or the Legal Action Group for further information (see appendix).

C) CIVIL LEGAL AID
Civil legal aid is also assessed according to your income and
savings. The Legal Aid Board will decide whether to grant you a
legal aid certificate. It may initially only enable you to take the
advice of a barrister (counsel). If the barrister says you have got
a case, this 'limitation' will be lifted and you should be able to
get legal aid all through the case. However, legal aid may be
granted without any limitations.
    Your income will be assessed for civil legal aid by the Depart-
ment of Social Security and this assessment will stand through
all the legal proceedings even if it reaches the House of Lords.

D) CRIMINAL LEGAL AID
This covers representation in criminal cases. Advice about
criminal matters can be obtained under the Green Form
Scheme (see appendix for address of the Legal Aid Board in
England and Wales where you can get further information
about legal aid).

11.2 Avenues for legal action and appeal
There is no decision of a local authority which is not open to
some sort of appeal or challenge through the courts, except for
traffic orders, although these could be challenged in the courts
on a point of law.

The content of the decision is not open to appeal unless it is so unreasonable that you could make a legal challenge on the grounds that no reasonable authority would make that decision. This section deals with some of the avenues for legal action and appeal against a local authority. As has been said, legal aid is only available to individuals and in taking legal action over, for example, flood damage in an area, the case has to be brought by named individuals affected.

A) JUDICIAL REVIEW

The main procedure is judicial review – only available to someone affected by a decision. Local authorities must make their decisions in a reasonable and lawful manner, and, if it can be shown that a local authority has improperly reached a decision, then the courts will not give effect to it. Also, if it is possible to show that a local authority has not or is not doing something Parliament has required it to do, like implementing a piece of legislation, the courts can order the local authority to take action. In some cases it may be possible to get judicial review against the termination of a grant if no reasons are given or incorrect evidence is used. This is being tested at the moment.

As explained above, you could get a legal aid certificate to enable you to get counsel's opinion to see if you have a case before legal aid is granted to take it through the courts.

B) TRIBUNALS

Many Acts of Parliament include a means of appeal against the decisions of a local authority of government body. This is often vested in a tribunal which is an administrative body, not a court of law, and is made up of ordinary members of the public appointed by the Secretary of State, usually made up of a legally qualified independent chair plus two members from a panel representing opposing interests. The tribunal will hear appeals and make a decision which the local authority will have to implement. Examples of tribunals which deal with local authority decisions are the Lands Tribunal (concerned with questions of compensation in relation to sales and purchase of land), the Industrial Tribunal (concerned with local authority staff matters), the Mental Health Review Tribunal (concerned with compulsory admissions to psychiatric hospitals). Section 11.1(b) explained how you can get legal advice and assistance to prepare you for a tribunal hearing but you cannot get legal costs for representation at the hearing, although you can take a friend or adviser with you to assist you or act on your behalf, or pay a solicitor to represent you.

However, you can get legal aid for a solicitor to represent you at a Mental Health Tribunal.

C) PLANNING APPPEALS AND INQUIRIES

(i) Local district authorities publish draft local plans for areas of their districts and these have to be shown to the public in the area concerned, and, in Wales, sent to the Secretary of State for Wales.

Members of the public can make objections to the plans. If there are objections, the Secretary of State will direct a public inquiry to be held, presided over by an inspector appointed by the Secretary of State. The inspector will report on his/her findings to the district authority who drew up the plan.

(ii) County councils, metropolitan districts and London boroughs publish Structure Plans for their areas. These are sent to the Secretary of State and are widely discussed by business, community interests and the public at large. The Secretary of State selects issues to be discussed arising from the public consultations and objections raised and appoints an inspector to undertake an Examination in Public (EIP) of the Plan. S/he reports back to the Secretary on the findings of the EIP.

(iii) Planning applications and appeal. If any aggrieved individual appeals against a decision made by the planning authority, concerning individual properties, pieces of land or areas of land or buildings, then a public inquiry is held. The only people who have the right to be heard are the appellant (the person appealing against the decision), the planning authority or the owner of the land. The inspector has the discretion to allow other people to be heard, eg local residents. The district councils are the planning authorities in these instances but they will consult a county council over a variety of proposed developments.

The county council can grant planning permission for its own developments, and, if they are contrary to their own structure plan, they must send a copy of the proposal to the Secretary of State who can 'call in' the application for his or her own determination. As explained in the introduction to this chapter, you can get legal aid and advice in helping you prepare for a planning appeal or inquiry, but not for representation at the hearing.

D) COMPULSORY PURCHASE ORDERS (CPOs)

There are far fewer CPOs of housing now than there were in the late sixties and seventies concerning housing redevelopment plans. Most CPOs by local authorities now concern acquisition of land for road developments. The local authority must advertise the fact that it intends to purchase a piece of land and submit the proposal to the Secretary of State for confirmation. If there are objections from any landowners, the Secretary of State must hold a public inquiry. It is up to his/her discretion whether or not to hold a public inquiry if anyone else objects who isn't a landowner. Often an application for planning permission will be submitted at the same time so that a public inquiry can deal with objections to the planning permisssion (if there are any) at the same time as the CPO objections.

E) CHILD CARE ORDERS

This is one of the major areas involving legal proceedings between a local authority (a county council, London borough or metropolitan district) and its residents. If the local authority thinks a child is in imminent danger, they can apply to the magistrate for the area in which the child is living for a 'place of safety order'. They do not have to notify the parents of the application and the court has the power to make a place of safety order for up to 28 days. All 'care' proceedings are dealt with by the Juvenile Court and often a place of safety order will be made until the next time the Juvenile Court meets.

If the local quthority wants to make a 'care order', the court has the power to make an order for separate legal representation if it feels there is a conflict between the interests of the child and the interests of the parent. This would mean that the child would be represented by a solicitor and would also have a Guardian ad Litem (usually a social worker, independent from the local authority and parents), and the parents could also have a solicitor representing them. The parents and the child (through his/her solicitor) can apply for legal aid to the Magistrates' Court. The court or Guardian ad Litem would make arrangements for the child to have a solicitor who would be taken from the Child Care Panel. (There are only a certain number of solicitors on this panel as they have to have dealt with child care cases and have experience in this field to be included).

If the child is in care and the local authority is refusing the parents access to the child, they can apply for legal aid to make an application to the court for access to be granted. The application for legal aid is decided by the Law Society but the proceedings are heard in the Magistrates' Court.

If the local authority thinks a child in care should be placed for adoption, the county council can apply to the county court to free the child for adoption. The parents can apply to the Law Society for legal aid, opposing this application.

Since the time of writing the Children's Act 1989 has been introduced with changes affecting parental and children's rights. For further information concerning the changes contact the Children's Legal Centre and the Family Rights Group (see appendix).

F) DAMAGES

Individuals can take action in the county court to claim damages for personal injuries which have been sustained due to faulty council property, eg if someone is injured through tripping on a faulty pavement, which is county council property, she or he can claim damages against the county council. If you go to a solicitor and ask them to sue for damages and the damage is assessed at more than £500, the council's insurers will pay both the damages and the legal costs. You can get legal aid to sue for damages, and you can go to the county court for claims of this kind up to a maximum of £5,000.

G) LICENSING

Local authorities are responsible for registering and licensing nurseries, childminders, private old people's homes, private nursing agencies, also entertainment centres where gaming licences are required, taxis, and flag days.

If a local authority turns down an application for a licence, the aggrieved person/organisation can appeal to the magistrates' court against the decision.

H) HOUSING

Local housing authorities have been taken to court by tenants of their properties under various housing Acts. Under section 11 of the Landlord and Tenant Act 1985, a local authority can be taken to court by a tenant if they can prove that the house is in need of structural repair, or that repairs to amenities (such as heating or WC) are necessary and the council has failed to do these repairs. You can get legal aid in taking action under this section of the Act. Under section 99 of the Public Health Act 1936, a local authority can be taken to court if there are defects in a tenant's house which are so bad that they could be a danger to health. You cannot get legal aid for taking action under this section, but if you won your case under section 99, you would get all you legal costs paid. A further Act which is used is the Housing Act 1985, section 604, when a tenant can attempt to prove that a house is so defective that it is unfit for human habitation. In that case you would be arguing that the state of the house falls below the basic minimum standards of fitness. You can get legal aid to take action under section 604.

It is advisable to make a written complaint to the local authority first (see chapter 10) if you think you could take action under any of these housing Acts. If you do not get a satisfactory response, and repairs are not carried out, then you can seek advice from an independant advice centre and from a solicitor. This is an area of law which few solicitors specialise in, so it would be worth contacting a housing action group such as Shelter (see appendix) for their advice. If you are a council tenant and you are being threatened with eviction under section 84 of the Housing Act 1985 by yur local housing authority, you can get legal aid to enable a solicitor to advise and represent you at the court hearings.

12
Your Rights to Personal Information

There is now a great deal of information kept by local authorities about us as citizens, consumers, clients and users of local authority services. Some of this is personal information about ourselves and you may wish to find out what the council knows about you so that you can check that it is correct and consider whether you think they need to keep this information about you on their computers.

This chapter helps identify which council departments may keep personal information about you, what registers and membership lists are likely to exist and what information is kept on them (eg poll tax).

It then goes on to tell you about your rights to personal information and protection of information about yourself via the Data Protection Act 1984, the Access to Personal Files Act 1987 and the poll tax register.

A) PERSONAL FILES (KEPT BY THE LOCAL AUTHORITY)
You may find that there are files kept on you by the local authority for the following reasons:
- you are an applicant on the housing waiting list
- you receive housing benefit
- you are a client of the social services department
- you are a student in adult or further education

- you are a school pupil

B) REGISTERS (KEPT BY THE LOCAL AUTHORITY)

Examples of these are the electoral register and the new poll tax (community charge) register.

C) MEMBERSHIPS

Local authorities will have you listed as members of libraries, leisure centres, adult education centres and classes.

12.1 Data Protection Act 1984

Since November 1987, new rights have been introduced with regard to personal information kept about you on computers. The above Act only applies to computer-kept information; it does not apply to information kept in manual files in filing cabinets. This is dealt with in 12.3 under the Access to Personal Files Act 1987.

Under the Data Protection Act 1984 you have the right to see the information you can be identified by. You can only have access to your own file, so that you cannot automatically see the file of, for example, your elderly parent. You can, however, see a file concerning your child.

We have already identified the sort of information the council is likely to keep on you. Much of that will be kept on computer. Councils are 'data users', which means they have to tell the Data Protection Registrar (see appendix for address) what kinds of files they have. This information is kept in a register held in public libraries, so you can find out what sort of files the council keeps and consider whether you are likely to be in any of them (eg as a housing benefit recipient). Some local authorities have data protection officers who may be able to assist you without you needing to go to the library and do your own research. You can ring the council and ask if they have a data protection officer.

HOW CAN YOU SEE YOUR FILE?

- You can write to the council and ask to see the file which concerns you.
- You may have to pay a fee, although some councils do not charge for the service.
- The council must reply to your request within 40 days. In

helping to understand your file entry, they must explain any information which may be in computer language.

- They do not have to give you access to information which concerns any proposals or intentions about your position, eg in relation to a decision about a service you hope to receive, or if you're an employee, whether you are likely to be made redundant. However, they should show you information containing opinions about you made by others. They do not have to reveal their sources of information about you.

- If you find you are having difficulties getting a response, or the council is being unhelpful in identifying or showing you your files, you can complain to the Registrar. You can also go to court to force the council to give you the information, but you would be wise to consult a solicitor first to see if he or she thinks you can win the case.

- If there is anything inaccurate in your file you have the right to get that mistake corrected. If you think you have lost out because of an inaccuracy, you can ask for compensation and/or a reconsideration of your case, eg if it involves financial loss or a place on a waiting list.

- Again, if you find you are having difficulties about getting the information put right or compensation, you can complain to the Registrar, and you still have the option of using the courts.

EXEMPTIONS TO THE ACT

It is possible that the council might have some personal information about you which they do not have to reveal because they come under certain exemptions to the Act. For example, the Secretary of State can order that access is limited to information kept in certain social work files. The regulations should be made clear to you. Also, if you did manage to see a file which contained information of this kind which was incorrect you can go to court and sue for damages.

The National Council for Civil Liberties has produced *Your Right to See Your File* (see appendix) which clearly lays out your rights under this Act. They advise you to go to the Registrar if you are having problems before going to the courts because they have powers to get information from users and they may be able to solve any problems you are having such as accuracy of information, compensation, etc.

For further information contact the Office of the Data Protection Registrar (see appendix).

12.2 Access to Personal Files Act 1987

This Act has come into force as a result of various circulars which lay our the regulations regarding your rights to see your personal files. This Act covers files which contain personal information which is not kept on computer (see 12.1 above). Anything which you can gain access to via the Data Protection Act is therefore excluded from the Access to Personal Files Act.

A) HOUSING RECORDS

Since 1 April 1989 you have the right to see your housing records. You only have the right to see information recorded after that date. However, some councils have been giving this right to tenants for many years. Regulations concerning school records come into force from September 1990. The government still has to announce regulations for students of higher education.

If you are a council tenant (or a tenant of a housing action trust), a former tenant or an applicant on a housing waiting list, or you have bought your council house, you should be able to see your file under this Act.

Similar to the Data Protection Act, the procedures for getting to see your file are as follows:

- You must apply in writing to see your file.
- You may be asked to pay a fee (up to £10.00), but some local authorities are not charging a fee.
- You will have to provide some identity in asking to see the file.
- The council must reply to your request within 40 days of your application.
- They must explain anything which you find unintelligible, eg as a result of jargon or abbreviations.

Like the Data Protection Act, you can only see information about yourself. You could see the records of another member of the family if they are living with you. If there is information about someone else in your records, the council can approach them to see if they would mind you seeing it if it is relevant to you. You should be able to have access to information which has been marked 'confidential', eg from a doctor, but the council could decide not to let you see information if they thought it would damage your physical or mental health (about yourself or someone in the family.)

If you do feel there is inaccurate information in your file, you can ask for it to be corrected. You may think an opinion has been formed on inaccurate information, and you can ask them to correct this. If they correct it they should change your filecopy and send you a copy of the corrected material. If they refuse to change it (because they disagree that they've got it wrong), they have got to put your views in the file alongside the information which you have disagreed about.

If you still disagree with the action taken about the information in your file/records, you can ask the council to review the decision. This would mean the case would be taken before a group of councillors for them to consider. You do not have a right of appeal to the courts. However, you could go to the local government ombudsman (see chapter 9). If you do have your case reviewed by councillors, you should be able to put your case in writing or speak to them at their meeting.

B) SOCIAL WORK RECORDS
Similar procedures apply to any records or files held by the social services department with some exceptions.

- You cannot see the files of other members of your family, only your own.
- You do not have to be told if the council has kept information from you which is 'exempt'.
- The council cannot withold information which reveals the identity of a social worker or someone who is paid by the social services department, eg a foster parent, unless that person would be put at serious risk from the disclosure.
- Like the housing records, information can be kept from you if the local authority thinks that your physical or mental health would be seriously affected by the information you have seen. With social work records the local authority can also take into account your emotional condition in deciding whether to withhold access to the files. The government says these grounds for withholding information must only be used in exceptional circumstances.

The Campaign for Freedom of Information campaigned for the Access to Personal Files Act and has produced an information kit which they update and a publications list on citizen action. (See appendix for address.) Information can also be provided on access to personal files by the National and Welsh Consumer Councils (see appendix).

12.3 Poll tax Register

The Local Government Act 1988 introduced the poll tax to replace the rates (see chapter 7) with this major change in the way we pay for our local government services coming into force from April 1990. As the poll tax is essentially a tax on the individual, not the property you own or live in, personal information has to be collected on those who are liable to pay the tax in order for local authorities to be able to charge them. Each local authority responsible for collecting the poll tax (district or borough) has to appoint a community charge registration officer (CCRO) who will have the responsibility of drawing up and maintaining a register of those people who are liable to pay the poll tax. (See chapter 7 for details of exemptions.)

The register was being drawn up in England and Wales at the time of writing (summer 1989). Initially the register was compiled by means of a canvass of households with forms being sent out to households for the occupants to complete by a certain date. Your name and address will appear in the register if you are liable to pay the tax from April 1990 and you completed one of these forms. If subsequently you moved or your circumstances changed which exempted you from paying the tax, you would have to inform the CCRO of the change in address or circumstance so that you would cease to be liable for poll tax at that address. The CCRO would mark this in the register marking the date on which your liability ceased. However, your name would still remain on the register for two years.

The CCROs initially used the old rates register and the electoral register to help them draw up their first canvass for the register. If they thought they had not drawn up a comprehensive list, they would start a 'secondary' investigation. (They may do this anyway.) There was a great deal of concern about these secondary investigations because they could involve CCROs getting access to personal information not relevant to the poll tax register, in their search. Also, your 'privacy' would be affected if the CCRO could identify you via your membership of a library or your position as a parent, in order to ensure you are on the poll tax register. The CCROs cannot be refused information by local authorities on any list, records or registers they might hold. CCROs also have the right to seek information from other CCROs and the electoral registration officer of each district. The Community Charge Regulations (Administration and Enforcement) 1989 empower CCROs to require local authorities to supply them with information, within 21 days, of the names and addresses of the people about whom the local authorities have information. This could include the names and addresses of parents of school children (if the LEA has kept that information). It can also include people on waiting lists (eg for housing) as well as membership lists. The local authority has no right to refuse to give the information.

It is unclear at the time of writing to what lengths the CCROs will pursue these sources. The Data Protection Act (see 12.1) gives you some protection as CCROs have to be registered as data users, so any information which is passed from the local authority to the CCRO has to comply with the Act. At the time of writing several CCROs were under inquiry for not registering under the Data Protection Act even though they were collecting personal information and processing it on computers. Out of 403 poll tax canvass forms requesting information only 37 satisfied the protection given by the Act (*The Guardian*, August 1989).

The guidelines given to CCROs on data protection suggest that CCROs should use their 'primary' canvass, the electoral register and the rating lists as their initial sources of information and only follow up secondary investigations in areas which are not considered 'sensitive'. Ministers have said that social work records should not be used in the investigations as this may deter people from seeking help.

WHAT WILL BE PUBLICLY AVAILABLE?
The poll tax register will be available for the public to see. It will only show the names and addresses of the people who are liable. The government agreed to allow those who live under the threat of violence to have their names and addresses removed (after pressure from Women's Aid). Local authorities have been told by the government that they cannot sell the registers.

YOUR RIGHTS AND THE REGISTER
You will have the right to get a statement from the CCRO showing what they have included in the Register about yourself. You can ask to see what other information they have about you (under the Data Protection Act). Remember that CCROs can pass information on to other CCROs without telling you.

You can appeal to the Valuation and Community Charge Tribunals if you disagree with an entry made about you in the register: the date you were registered, information contained and anything which affects your liability to pay. See *Privacy and the Poll Tax: Your Rights and the Law in England and Wales* (NCCL) and *Responding to Rate Reform* (NCVO) (see appendix).

13
Local Authorities Associations – What Are They and How to Use Them

This chapter will explain the structure, responsibilities and role of local authorities associations and will consider how you can use them for obtaining and circulating information and for contacting groups of councillors with special interests.

13.1 What is the role of local authorities associations?

Local authorities associations bring together local authorities which are involved with the same level and type of local council throughout England and Wales; for example, the Association of County Councils (ACC) brings together the counties in England and Wales (see chapter 2). Membership is open to all the local authorities in a particular 'tier', and the majority will join an association. Some local authorities can belong to more than one association; for example, Welsh counties may belong to the ACC and to the Welsh Counties Committee (WCC).

The associations are organisations which aim to promote the interests of their member authorities. They will represent their views in Parliament in relation to laws affecting local government, and they will inform and advise their members about the implications of changes in government policy and laws.

They will bring together people with common interests, eg social services, housing or education, to discuss current changes, policy developments and directions, and may produce reports on particular issues and organise conferences about particular areas of concern. These are often open to other organisations sharing the same concerns, including the voluntary sector, as well as to their own members.

At any one time, the associations may be 'politically controlled' (see chapter 4) by one political party, but this obviously changes as the political control of the individual authorities changes.

Members of the associations will have representatives serving on the main association committees. These will be elected councillors, but the paid officers of councils often also play a considerable role in the associations' business servicing or advising the committees. The associations are financed by subscriptions paid by the member authorities.

13.2 Who are they?

In chapter 2 we described the structure and responsibilities of local government in England and Wales. The associations' membership corresponds to this structure in the following way:

A) THE NON-METROPOLITAN AREAS

County councils in England and Wales are eligible for membership of the Association of County Councils (ACC). County councils in Wales can also be members of the Welsh Counties Committee (WCC). District councils in England and Wales can be members of the Association of District Councils (ADC). In Wales district councils can also be members of the Committee of Welsh District Councils.

B) THE METROPOLITAN AREAS

All metropolitan districts and London boroughs, the ILEA, and the City of London are eligible for membership of the Association of Metropolitan Authorities (AMA). The joint authorities set up after abolition of the GLC and MCCs (see chapter 2) can also take up limited membership.

C) LONDON
As well as being able to join the AMA. London boroughs and the City of London can also join London-based authority associations. There are two operating, the Association of London Authorities (ALA) and the London Boroughs Association (LBA). London boroughs tend to belong to one or the other.

D) JOINT AUTHORITIES
As has been said, these can join the AMA as corporate members.

E) PARISH, TOWN AND COMMUNITY COUNCILS
Parish, town and community councils can join the National Association of Local Councils (NALC). There is also a Welsh Association of Community and Town Councils to which Welsh town and community councils can belong (as well as or instead of NALC). In addition, there are other local authority associations, such as the National Association of Local Government Women's Committees (see appendix).

13.3 What can the associations offer you?
Local authority associations often have close links with voluntary organisations and it is useful to keep them informed of your work and activities; sending them your annual reports and informing them of your comments on matters which affect local government and the voluntary sector. For example, if you have produced a report on the funding problems of a particular voluntary organisation, send copies to all the local authority associations in your area. If you produce a report on housing which has some comments on general housing policy, send it to the ADC or CWDC, the AMA, the ALA and the LBA. As one of their functions is to lobby the government about the effects of laws on local authorities, they will often welcome comments from voluntary organisations which can assist them in this task. You can also ask to meet members of a local authority association, or to discuss your ideas or problems with the officers of the association so that they can advise their members of your views.

Unless you are a national organisation, it may be difficult to make constructive contact with a large local authorities association. It may be more effective for individual organisations to contact the NCVO or WCVA to ask them to raise issues or points on your behalf as they have regular meetings with the associations. This may also be a useful avenue for national organisations in addition to their own lobbying of the associations.

Most associations have journals or newsletters which you could subscribe to, and you could ask if they would receive an article about your organisation.

If you are holding a conference you could invite members of the association to attend. You could also write to the associations and ask them to inform you of any conferences they are organising which may be relevant to your interests.

Associations will have published reports, leaflets and booklets on matters of concern to local government. It is worth asking for the associations' publications list to see if there is anything which will be of use to you in your work. (See appendix for the addresses of all local authority associations.)

APPENDIX

USEFUL ADDRESSES AND PUBLICATIONS

Useful addresses

Throughout the guide, various organisations and publications have been mentioned which can provide further information. This appendix lists these organisations in alphabetical order, and gives details of the publications recommended in the guide.

Campaign for Freedom of Information
3 Endsleigh Street
London WC1H 0DD
Tel. 01-278 9686

Children's Legal Centre
20 Compton Terrace
London N1 2UN
Tel. 01-359 6251

Community Rights Project
15/17 Red Cross Way
London SE1 1TB
Tel. 01-407 2397

Directory of Social Change
Radius Works
Back Lane
London NW3 1HL
Tel. 01-435 8171

Family Rights Group
6–9 Manor Gardens
Holloway Road
London N7 6LA
Tel. 01-263 4016/9724

Federation of Independent Advice Centres
13 Stockwell Road
London SW9 9AU
Tel. 01-274 1839

also at:
4th Floor
Concourse House
Lime Street
Liverpool 1
Tel. 051-709 7444

Law Centres Federation
Rooms 54–55
1 Albert Street
Birmingham B4 7TX
Tel. 021-236 5610

also at:
Duchess House
18–19 Warren Street
London W1P SDB
Tel. 01-387 8570

Law Society
113 Chancery Lane
London WC2A 1PL
Tel. 01-242 1222

Legal Action Group
242 Pentonville Road
London N1 9UN
Tel. 01-833 2931/2/3

Legal Aid Board
Legal Aid Head Office
Newspaper House
8–16 Great New Street
London EC4A 3BN
Tel. 01-353 7411

*Local Government Information
Unit*
(LGIU)
1–5 Bath Street
London EC1 9QQ
Tel. 01-608 1051

*Local Government Training
Board*
4th Floor
Avondale House
Avondale Centre
Luton LV1 2TS
Tel. 0582-451166

*London Borough Grants
Scheme*
PO Box 57
Twickenham
Middlesex TW1 3A2
Tel. 01-891 5021

London Strategic Policy Unit
Middlesex House
20 Vauxhall Bridge Road
London SW1V 2SB
Tel. 01-633 5944

(Including *Police Monitoring
and Research Group*)

*London Voluntary Services
Council*
68 Charlton Street
London NW1 1JR
Tel. 01-388 0241

*National Association of Citizens
Advice Bureaux*
115–123 Pentonville Road
London N1 9LZ
Tel. 01-833 2181

National Consumer Council
20 Grosvenor Gardens
London SW1W 0DH
Tel. 01-730 3469

*National Council for Civil
Liberties*
21 Tabard Street
London SE1 4LA
Tel. 01-403 3888

National Council for Voluntary Organisations
26 Bedford Square
London WC1B 3HU
Tel. 01-636 4066

Office of the Data Protection Registrar
Springfield House
Water Lane
Wilmslow
Cheshire SK9 5AX
Tel. 0625-535777

Scottish Council for Voluntary Action
18/19 Claremont Crescent
Edinburgh EH7 4QD
Tel. 031-556 3882

Shelter – National Campaign for the Homeless
88 Old Street
London EC1V 9HU
Tel. 01-253 0202

or Shelter (Wales)
57 Walters Road
Swansea, West Glamorgan
Tel. 0792-469400

Special Needs Housing Advisory Service
16–18 Strutton Ground
London SW1P 2HP
Tel. 01-222 5544

also at:
The Maltings
East Tyndall Street
Cardiff CF1 5EA
Tel. 0222-492746

Tenant Participation Advisory Service (TPAS) (England)
48 The Crescent
Salford
Manchester M5 4NY
Tel. 061-745 7903

TPAS (Wales)
9 Womanby Street
Cardiff CF1 2BR
Tel. 0222-237303

TPAS (Scotland)
4 St Andrews Street
Glasgow G15PN
Tel. 041-552 3633

Wales Council for Voluntary Action
Llys Ifor
Crescent Road
Caerphilly CF8 1XL
Tel. 0222-869224

Welsh Consumer Council
Castle Buildings
Womanby Street
Cardiff CF1 2BN
Tel. 0222-396056

Local authority associations

Association of District Councils
9 Buckingham Gate
London SW1E 6LE
Tel. 01-828 7931

Association of County Councils
Eaton House
66a Eaton Square

London SW1 9BH
Tel. 01-235 1200

*Association of London
Authorities*
36 Old Queen Street
London SW1H 9JF
Tel. 01-222 7799

*Association of Metropolitan
Authorities*
35 Great Smith Street
London SW1P 3BJ
Tel. 01-222 8100

Council of Welsh Districts
10/11 Raleigh Walk
Atlantic Wharf
Cardiff CF1 5LN
Tel. 0222-462 722

London Boroughs Association
Westminster City Hall
Victoria Street
London SW1E 6QP
Tel. 01-798 2736

*National Association of Local
Councils*
108 Great Russell Street
London WC1B 3LD
Tel. 01-637 1865/6/7/8

*National Association of Local
Government Women's
Committees*
Pankhurst Centre
60–62 Nelson Street
Chorlton-on-Medlock
Manchester M13 9WP
Tel. 061-274 3684

*Welsh Association of Com-
munity and Town Councils*
Pen Roc
Rhodfa'n Mon
Aberystwyth SY23 2A2
Tel. 0970-612801

Welsh Counties Committee
County Hall
Mid Glamorgan County
Council
Cathays Park
Cardiff CF1 3NE
Tel. 0222-820094

Useful publications

Association of London Authorities. *London Government Directory*, ALA, 1988.

Aughton, Henry. *Housing Finance: A Basic Guide*, Shelter, 1986.

Bailey, Ron. *Guide to Councillors' Rights to Information*, Community Rights Project, 1985.

Clark, John. *Powers and Constitution of Local Councils* (available in English and Welsh), National Association of Local Councils, 1987.

Community Rights Project. *Wallchart on the Access to Information Act*, Community Rights Project, 1985.

Community Service Volunteers. *Local Government: Making It Work for You*, CSV, 1986.

Dawson, Catherine. *Partners in Learning: A Guide to the Provisions of the Education Act 1988 Regarding Adult Education and Voluntary Groups*, NCVO, 1990.

Esam, Peter. *LGIU Guide to the Poll Tax*, Local Government Information Unit, 1988.

Fielding, Nick and Gutch, Richard. *Contracting In or Out: The Legal Context, Guidance Notes on Contracting for Voluntary Groups No. 1*, 1989.

Fraser, Ross. *A Tenants' Guide to Tenants' Choice* and *A Guide to Voluntary Transfer*, TPAS and the National Consumer Council, 1990.

Gutch, Richard. *The Conduct of Local Government: A Guide to the Local Government and Housing Act 1989*, NCVO, 1990.

Gutch, Richard. *The Contract Culture: The Challenge for Voluntary Organisations, Guidance Notes on Contracting for Voluntary Groups No. 2*, National Council for Voluntary Organisations, 1989.

Gutch, Richard and Grace, Clive. *Getting in on the Act*. National Council for Voluntary Organisations, 2nd edn, 1990.

Gutch, Richard, Percival, Richard and Miliband, David. *Publish and Still Not Be Damned: A Guide for Voluntary Groups on the Provisions of the 1986 and 1988 Local Government Acts regarding Political Publicity and Promotion of Homosexuality*, National Council for Voluntary Organisations, 1989.

Gutch, Richard and Young, K. *Partners or Rivals?* Local Government Training Board, 1988.

Hutt, Jane. *Responding to Rate Reform: A Guide to the Local Government Finance Act 1988*, NCVO, 1988.

Jones, Maggie. *Government Grants: A Guide for Voluntary Organisations*, Bedford Square Press, 5th edition, 1988.

Jones, Maggie. *Voluntary Organisations and the Media*, Bedford Square Press, 2nd edition, 1990.

Kunz, C., Jones, R. and Spencer, K. *Bidding for Change*, Birmingham Settlement and Community Projects Foundation, 1989.

Law Centres Federation. *Law Centres Federation Journal*.

Local Government Information Unit. *LGIU Bulletin* (monthly), LGIU (includes Information Briefings, Local Link, Trade Union Briefing, Women's News.

National Council for Civil Liberties. *Your Right to See Your File: Civil Liberty Briefing Note No. 8*, NCCL, 1987.

National Council for Civil Liberties. *Privacy and the Poll Tax: Your Rights and the Law in England and Wales*, 1989.

National Council for Voluntary Organisations. *Contracting – In or Out?*

National Council for Voluntary Organisations. *Negotiating Grants*, Community Care Project, 1987.

National Council for Voluntary Organisations and National Association of Community Relations Councils. *Section 11: Funding for Black and Ethnic Minorities and Guidance Notes for Voluntary Groups*, NCVO/NACRCs, 1988.

Norton, Michael. *Raising Money for Government*, Directory of Social Change, 1985.

Reason, Jacki. *Who's Who in London Government?*, Local Government Training Board, 1985.

Shelter. *The Housing Act 1988*, Shelter, 1989.

Stewart, John. *The Management of Hung Authorities*, Local Government Training Board, 1985.

Taylor, Marilyn. *Into the 1990s. Voluntary Organisations and the Public Sector*, NCVO/RIPA, 1988.

Thompson, Catherine and Hadley, Jane. *Negotiating Grants: Issues for Local Authorities and Voluntary Groups*, National Council for Voluntary Organisations, 1987.

Index

All books are available through bookshops. In case of difficulty books can be ordered by post direct from Plymbridge Distributors Ltd, Estover Road, Plymouth PL6 7PZ (tel. 0752-705251) adding 12½% to total value of order for post and packing (minimum 30p).